Yorkshire

AA Publishing

Produced by AA Publishing
© The Automobile Association 1998
Maps © The Automobile Association 1998

First published 1998

All rights reserved. No part of this publication may be reproduced, stored in a retrieval system, or transmitted in any form or by any means – electronic, photocopying, recording or otherwise – unless the written permission of the publisher has been obtained beforehand.

Published by AA Publishing (a trading name of Automobile Association Developments Limited, whose registered office is Norfolk House, Priestley Road, Basingstoke, Hampshire RG24 9NY; registered number 1878835).

ISBN 0 7495 1816 2

A CIP catalogue record for this book is available from the British Library.

The contents of this book are believed correct at the time of printing. Nevertheless, the publishers cannot be held responsible for any errors or omissions or for changes in the details given in this book or for the consequences of any reliance on the information provided by the same. Material from this book has been previously published by AA Publishing in various publications.

Colour separation by Pace Colour Ltd, Southampton

Printed and bound in Italy by Stige, Turin

Find out more about AA Publishing and the wide range of services the AA provides by visiting our Web site at www.theaa.co.uk.

YORKSHIRE

Foremost among Yorkshire's many attractions are its two national parks – the North York Moors and the Yorkshire Dales. The landscape of the Dales was formed by water wearing deep into the limestone creating gorges and waterfalls, wide valleys and slow rivers. Lush valleys give way to crags, grassland and moors on the hilltops. The rolling hills of the North York Moors are ablaze with purple heather in late summer and there are green valleys, rock-strewn streams and forests. Busy seaside resorts, market towns and pretty villages have an appeal all of their own.

Between the national parks are the ancient settlements of Ripon and Richmond. Ripon is dominated by its beautiful cathedral, while Richmond's market place is overlooked by the keep of its castle. Near by are fascinating villages, delightful countryside and Fountains Abbey, one of the best-preserved monasteries in Europe. The historic city of York, with its ancient walls and mighty church, is to the south-east.

The Industrial Revolution changed the face of Yorkshire when the great cities of Sheffield, Leeds and Bradford developed around the coalfields. Though these areas may not immediately suggest themselves as tourist attractions, many have been revitalised and have much to offer – proud museums to their industrial heritage, imaginative uses for industrial sites, lively arts and entertainments and superb sporting venues.

Whether travelling by train on the scenic Settle to Carlisle or Pickering to Grosmont lines, by car along the narrow roads that climb and twist up to a breath-taking summit, or on foot along the Pennine Way, the natural beauty of the landscape is enhanced by its history – standing stones on remote moorland, Roman roads and forts, medieval abbeys in lush valleys and castles presiding over the hills and rivers.

gazetteer

ALDBOROUGH – AYSGARTH

ALDBOROUGH

NORTH YORKSHIRE. VILLAGE OFF B6265, 1 MILE (1.5KM) SE OF BOROUGHBRIDGE

Roman Town

SE OF BOROUGHBRIDGE, ON MINOR ROAD OFF B6265 WITHIN 1 MILE (1.5KM) OF JUNCTION OF A1 & A6055
TEL: 01423 322768

AYSGARTH

NORTH YORKSHIRE. VILLAGE ON A684, 7 MILES (11KM) W OF LEYBURN

Aysgarth Upper Falls

▶ The village stands on the foundations of a thriving Roman town. The maypole on the village green is still used for traditional May Day dances, and a cross commemorates a battle fought here in 1322.

▶ The pretty present-day village occupies the site of the northernmost civilian Roman town in Britain, with houses, courts, a forum and a temple, surrounded by a wall 9 feet (3m) thick and 20 feet (6m) high. All that can be seen today are two mosaic pavements, the position of the wall and excavated objects in the small museum. The site is in the care of English Heritage.
  Open Apr–Oct, daily.

▶ Just outside the village are the impressive Aysgarth Falls, which tumble over limestone terraces in a system which extends for about a mile (1.5km). Below 18th-century Aysgarth bridge is Yore Mill which houses a collection of horse-drawn vehicles. St Andrew's Church above the mill has a rood screen and an abbot's stall from Jervaulx Abbey. The Yorkshire Dales National Park information centre is near by.
  (See also Cycle ride: Wensleydale and the Yorkshire Dales, page 27.)

AYSGARTH – BEMPTON

gazetteer

▶ This visitor centre for the Yorkshire Dales National Park offers maps, guides, walks and local information. Displays explain the history and natural history of the area.
   Open Apr–Oct, daily. Nov–Mar limited weekend opening.

▶ The Grade II Listed building at Aysgarth Falls, built in 1784, houses a varied collection of Victorian horse-drawn vehicles including a mail coach, a hearse, a 'haunted' carriage and a fire engine all in their original condition. There is also an exhibition of handmade scale models of American and traditional English coaches and carriages.
   Open all year, daily. Closed 24 Dec–12 Jan.

▶ This attractive old market town gained its charter in 1251 and has a market cross which dates from the 14th century. Bedale Hall, a Georgian mansion with ornate plaster ceilings, now houses the district council offices and a small museum. The Church of St Gregory has a fortified tower and incorporates architectural styles from 1000 to 1500. To the north west the restored buildings and machinery of Crakehall Watermill now produce wholemeal flour. Thorpe Perrow Arboretum, to the south of Bedale, contains over 1,000 species of plants and trees in 85 acres (34ha) of gardens and woodland.

▶ Housed in a building of 17th-century origin, with Palladian and Georgian extensions, the centre of this fascinating little museum is the Bedale fire engine dated 1742. Old documents, photographs, clothing, toys, craft tools and household utensils give an absorbing picture of the life of ordinary people.
   Open Etr–Sep, most days. Oct–Etr, limited opening.

▶ Bempton is an attractive village near the North Sea coast. St Michael's Church has some interesting early 13th-century features, including a screen incorporating the royal arms. A road from the village leads to Bempton Cliffs and the RSPB centre, where there is car parking.

▶ The reserve, situated on the spectacular chalk cliffs which stretch from Flamborough Head to Speeton, is one of the best sites in England to observe thousands of nesting seabirds at close quarters. The viewing platforms, which overlook the cliffs, are best visited from April to July when enormous numbers of seabirds, including guillemots, razorbills, kittiwakes, fulmars, herring gulls and several pairs of shag can be seen. This is the only gannetry on the mainland of England, and it is growing annually. Terns, skuas and shearwaters are among the many

---

National Park Centre
TEL: 01969 663424

Yorkshire Carriage Museum
YORE MILL, 1¾ MILES (3KM) E ON UNCLASSIFIED ROAD N OF A684. TURN RIGHT AT PALMER FLATT HOTEL, MUSEUM 300 YARDS (274.4M)
TEL: 01969 663399

BEDALE
NORTH YORKSHIRE. SMALL TOWN ON A684, 7 MILES (11KM) SW OF NORTHALLERTON

Bedale Hall
ON A684 1½ MILES (2.5KM) W OF A1 AT LEEMING BAR
TEL: 01677 424604

BEMPTON
EAST RIDING OF YORKSHIRE. VILLAGE OFF B1229, 3 MILES (5KM) N OF BRIDLINGTON

RSPB Nature Reserve
TAKE CLIFF ROAD FROM B1229, BEMPTON VILLAGE
TEL: 01262 851179

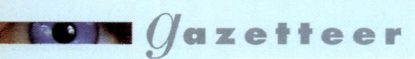

BEMPTON–BEVERLEY

migrants which pass offshore. Wheatears, ring ouzels, merlins and bluethroats frequent the clifftop on migration. Grey seal and porpoise are sometimes seen from the cliffs.

Visitor centre open daily, Apr–Sep.

BENINGBROUGH HALL
NORTH YORKSHIRE. OFF A19, 8 MILES (13KM) NW OF YORK. ENTRANCE AT NEWTON LODGE
TEL: 01904 470666

▶ Beningbrough (National Trust) was built around 1716, and its structure has hardly been altered since then. It houses 100 pictures from the National Portrait Gallery in London. Perhaps the finest feature of the house is the Great Staircase, built of oak with wide parquetried treads and delicate balusters carved to imitate wrought iron. Ornately carved wood panelling is a feature of several of the rooms, notably the drawing room. The other side of country house life can be seen in the restored Victorian laundry, which has its original stoves, drying racks and other equipment. The gardens include formal areas, a conservatory and a wilderness play area.

Open Apr–Oct, certain days.

BEVERLEY
EAST RIDING OF YORKSHIRE. TOWN ON A164, 8 MILES (13KM) N OF HULL

▶ Beverley, a very pretty market town with elegant Georgian terraces and promenades, was described by Sir John Betjeman as 'a place for walking in and living in', and which the National Council of Archaeology has declared 'so splendid and precious that the ultimate responsibility for it should be a national concern'.

The Minster, begun in 1220, is a splendid example of Gothic architecture. Its twin bell towers can be seen for miles across the flat countryside and its interior is packed with the monumental art of some 700 years. Beverley's other great church, St Mary's, was built in the 13th century with money raised by the ancient guilds which represented the town's cloth-weaving, tanning and dyeing trades. Between the two churches is the town's market centre, which also separates the Saturday and Wednesday market places.

Art Gallery
CHAMPNEY RD
TEL: 01482 883903

▶ Local antiquities, Victorian bygones and china are displayed along with pictures of Beverley and other works of art. Notable among these is the bust of Sir Winston Churchill by Bryant Baker of New York. Solo art exhibitions are held here.

Open all year, most days.

Guildhall
REGISTER SQ
TEL: 01482 867430

▶ The Guildhall was established in 1500 and then rebuilt in handsome classical style in 1762. It is now used as a county court and Mayor's Parlour, but can be visited for its notable ceiling painting in the courtroom, its display of civic regalia, ancient charters and other treasures. A guide service is available.

Open all year, daily. Closed Sun, Oct–Etr.

BEVERLEY—BOLTON CASTLE

gazetteer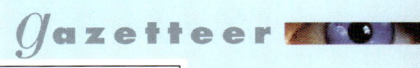

- The museum tells the story of army transport from horse-drawn waggons to the recent Gulf conflict: everything from prototype vehicles to Montgomery's Rolls-Royce and the last Blackburn Beverley aircraft – the museum's largest exhibit. Exhibitions include 'Women at the Wheel' which shows the role of women in military transport. A special area for children has a junior assault course and an adventure play area.

  Open all year, daily. Closed 24–26 Dec.

Museum of Army Transport
FLEMINGATE
TEL: 01482 860445

- Lord Scrope was Richard II's Chancellor – although he did not hold office for very long, for he was outspoken about the way in which the young king squandered treasury funds. Several times he refused to set his seal to some of the king's more lavish bouts of spending. Before Scrope resigned his office at Richard's Court, he was granted a licence to upgrade his manor house in Wensleydale to a castle. He hired a master mason called John Lewyn, who had also worked on the great castles of Raby and Dunstanburgh, to build him a formidable square fortress.

  Bolton Castle is built in the form of a quadrangle, with strong towers at each corner. There was only one entry into the courtyard, and that was through a vaulted passage with a portcullis at each end, also protected by a guard house. Inside the courtyard, every door that led into the buildings had its own portcullis. The buildings themselves were constructed of local stone, although the decorative arches over some of the doors and windows were made of the more expensive freestone from a quarry a little further away.

  During the Civil War the castle was besieged for more than a year by Cromwell's troops, and finally taken in 1645.

  Open Mar–Nov, daily.

BOLTON CASTLE
NORTH YORKSHIRE. CASTLE OFF A684, 5 MILES (8KM) W OF LEYBURN
TEL: 01969 623981

Sturdy Bolton Castle was built around 1379

Walk

BOLTON PRIORY

This is a walk with lots of variety – a ruined 12th-century priory, riverside areas with a footbridge, stepping stones, stretches of sand and pretty woodland paths with fine views. It is also relatively sheltered, making it an ideal winter walk.

Grid ref: SE071539
INFORMATION
The walk is about 2½ miles (4km) long.
Mainly on woodland or riverside paths, two short but easy climbs and a section above the river.
No road walking.
A few stiles.
Refreshment facilities in Bolton Abbey village; cafeteria, restaurant, snacks and ice cream at Cavendish Pavilion (seasonal).
Extensive grassy picnic areas by the priory footbridge and along the riverside.
Toilets at Bolton Abbey car park and Cavendish Pavilion.

START
Bolton Abbey village can be reached from Skipton (6 miles/9.5km west) on the A59, turning north at Bolton Bridge along the B6160, or from Ilkley via the A65, joining the B6160 at Addingham. There is a large, well-signed car park (charge) at Bolton Bridge.

DIRECTIONS
From the top end of the car park, pass the Information Board, turning right into the village. Cross the B6160 (very busy at times) to the hole in the wall opposite, which is the footpath into the Bolton Abbey Estate.

Go down the steps towards the riverside and head towards the wooden footbridge and stepping stones. Cross the bridge (the stepping stones should be avoided unless the river is very low) and ascend the hillside to reach a higher level path through the woods. Keep on the main path through the woods, eventually descending to a stile and rounding the hillside to join the lane from Storiths. Keep ahead to cross the stream at

The beautiful 12th-century ruins of Bolton Priory

BOLTON PRIORY

Walk

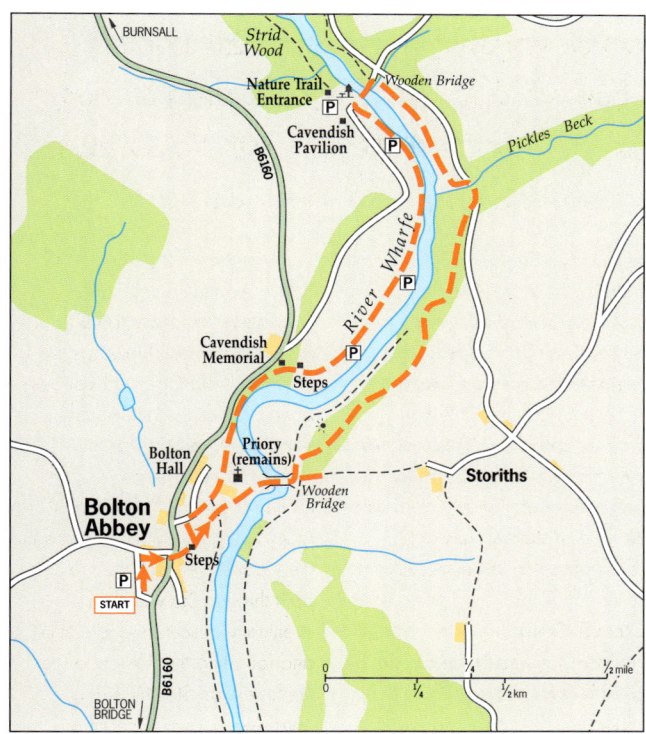

Pickles Gill by the footbridge to the right (or stepping stones ahead). Turn left alongside the stream to a stile which leads to the riverside path and then a second stile to cross the wooden bridge at the Cavendish Pavilion. (The walk can be extended at this point into the Strid Wood Nature Trails; a free map is available at the entrance).

From the Cavendish Pavilion, go back along the riverside past the parking areas, following the curve of the river to the right where, on the hillside, a narrow path leads to steps and a stile then meets the road by the Cavendish Memorial. Keep left along the path parallel to the road and go through a gate to the entrance of Bolton Priory church.

Maintain your direction along the church drive, past the rectory, taking the stile left to a path over the field, rejoining the path to the hole in the wall to return to the village centre.

Bolton Priory

The priory was founded by a group of Augustinian canons, who moved here from Embsay, near Skipton, around 1154. The church (still in use) and most of the ruins date from the 12th to the 15th century, the newest part being Prior Moone's western tower which was never completed. The roof is a very recent addition. Bolton Hall was converted from the former gatehouse in the 18th century: the rectory was once a grammar school, endowed by the 17th-century scientist, Robert Boyle (of Boyle's Law fame).

The Legend of the White Doe of Rylstone

During Elizabethan times an abortive rising against the queen spelled disaster for the Nortons of nearby Rylstone Hall, resulting in imprisonment or death for most of the family. A surviving sister, Emily, would walk 6 miles (9.5km) across the moors to visit her brother's grave in Bolton Priory churchyard, taking with her the little white doe that had been a gift from her brother. Long after her death the white doe would still be seen wandering around the gravestones.

WHAT TO LOOK OUT FOR

Trout can often be seen from the footbridge by the priory, and birdlife includes mallard, dippers and grey wagtails along the river, blue tits and chaffinches in the woods.

gazetteer

BOROUGHBRIDGE—BRADFORD

BOROUGHBRIDGE
NORTH YORKSHIRE. SMALL TOWN ON B6265, 6 MILES (9.5KM) SE OF RIPON

BOSTON SPA
WEST YORKSHIRE. VILLAGE ON A659, 4 MILES (6KM) NW OF TADCASTER

BRADFORD
WEST YORKSHIRE. CITY OFF M62, 8 MILES (13KM) W OF LEEDS

▶ Boroughbridge, once an important coaching stop on the Great North Road, is now bypassed by the A1. The town has a mixture of Regency, Georgian and Victorian architecture with an elaborate fountain dominating St James' Square. The nearby legendary Devil's Arrows are three stone monuments dating from 2000 BC, the largest is 30ft (9m) high. Market day is Thursday.

▶ A pretty place on the River Wharfe, with many Georgian houses surviving from the time when the spa was a popular resort. The growth of the town began in 1774 when the discovery of a spring was made by a local labourer called John Shires. From then until well into the 19th century the town was known as Thorp Spa.

▶ In 1801 Bradford was a country market town with 6,000 inhabitants. Thirty years later the population had grown to 97,000 as the textile industry transformed the town, and by the end of the century Bradford was known as the wool capital of the world. The prosperous Victorians backed a massive building programme using local Pennine stone, creating splendid public buildings, German merchants built ornate warehousing in the area of the town known as Little Germany, mills were modelled on Italian palaces and impressive private homes sprang up. Today over 4,000 buildings in the Bradford district are listed for their architectural or historical significance.

Heavy engineering, print and packaging firms, financial and export businesses thrived upon Bradford's success in the textile industry for many years, until the 1960s and 1970s when this core trade declined sharply. Bradford then set out to attract new investment and to launch the town and its district as a tourist destination, which it has done with remarkable success. Its large Asian population has provided one of Bradford's most popular features, and the town makes much of its reputation for having the finest curry houses in the country.

Although Bradford is less dependent on textile production these days, it still plays a vital role in the local economy. The mills are highly mechanised and specialise in top-quality fabrics and yarns, many of which are exported to Japan and Europe. The mill shops are also a great attraction, selling their produce to the public at wholesale prices.

The National Museum of Film, Photography and Television, in the centre of the town, houses an IMAX screen which stands five storeys high. Bradford's Colour Museum explains, amongst other things, how the world looks to animals, and reflects the town's industrial past showing how colour is used in textiles and printing. The Industrial Museum chronicles the history of the town's textile and manufacturing industry. Treadwell's Art Mill in the historic quarter of Little Germany

BRADFORD gazetteer

Bradford city centre

contains the world's biggest collection of Super Humanism art and sculpture. The Alhambra Theatre, a provincial Edwardian theatre, is a major venue for touring productions by the English National Ballet, Scottish Opera, Opera North and the Royal Shakespeare Company.

▶ A classic West Yorkshire manor house, complete with a galleried 'housebody' (hall), Bolling Hall dates mainly from the 17th century but has medieval and 18th-century sections. Room settings display period furniture and items relating to local history. There are panelled rooms, plasterwork in original colours, heraldic glass and a rare Chippendale bed. There is also a 'ghost room'.

Open all year, most days. Closed Mon (ex BH), Tue, Good Fri, 25 & 26 Dec.

Bolling Hall
BOWLING HALL RD. 1 MILE
(1.5KM) FROM CITY CENTRE
OFF A650
TEL: 01274 723057

▶ Moorside Mills, an original spinning mill, is now part of a museum that brings vividly to life the story of the woollen industry in Bradford. The magnificent machinery that once converted raw wool into the finest cloth is on display and the mill yard rings with the sound of iron on stone as shire horses pull trams, haul buses or give rides. The mill owner's house beside the mill is also open and gives an idea of domestic life around 1900, and the back-to-back cottages of Gaythorne Row, just across the street, show how the textile workers would have lived from the late-19th century until the 1950s. There are changing exhibitions and daily demonstrations.

Open all year, most days. Closed Mon (ex BH).

Bradford Industrial Museum and Horses at Work
MOORSIDE RD, ECCLESHILL.
OFF A658
TEL: 01274 631756

BRADFORD—BRAMHAM PARK

Cartwright Hall Art Gallery
LISTER PARK. 1 MILE (1.5KM) FROM CITY CENTRE ON A650
TEL: 01274 493313

▶ Built in dramatic Baroque style in 1904, this art gallery has permanent collections of 19th- and 20th-century British art, contemporary prints, and older works by British and European masters, including the *Brown Boy* by Reynolds.

Open all year, most days. Closed Mon (ex BH), Good Fri, 25 & 26 Dec.

Colour Museum
1 PROVIDENCE ST. FROM CITY CENTRE FOLLOW SIGNS B6144 (HAWORTH) THEN FOLLOW BROWN TOURIST INFORMATION SIGNS
TEL: 01274 390955

▶ Britain's only museum of colour comprises two galleries packed with visitor-operated exhibits demonstrating the effects of light and colour, including optical illusions, and the story of dyeing and textile printing. It even offers the chance to take charge of a modern dye-making factory and to try computer-aided exterior and interior design. There is a programme of special exhibitions and events.

Open all year, most days. Closed Sun, Mon & BH.

National Museum of Photography, Film & Television
PICTUREVILLE
TEL: 01274 727488

▶ The National Museum of Photography, Film and Television portrays the past, present and future of the media using interactive displays and dramatic reconstructions – visitors can ride on a magic carpet, become a newsreader for the day or have a go at vision mixing. Action Replay, the museum's own theatre company, regularly performs highlights from the galleries. At the heart of the museum is IMAX, Britain's largest cinema screen, which is over five storeys high. Vast, brilliant images sweep you into another world, exploring the realms of space and the depths of the ocean or indeed any subject big enough to be turned into this extraordinary experience.

Open all year, most days. Closed Mon.

Transperience
TRANSPERIENCE WAY
TEL: 01274 690909

▶ At Transperience visitors can travel on historic vehicles on the Translink system and delve into the history of public transport, to feel, hear and actually smell what was once considered to be the height of innovation. Test your hand at driving a tram, trolleybus, motorbus or train on the vehicle simulators. There are high-tech multi-screen productions featuring state-of-the-art lighting and animations, five exhibition halls to explore, an an adventure park for children in the 15-acre (6ha) all-weather site.

Open all year, daily. Closed 25–26 Dec.

BRAMHAM PARK
WEST YORKSHIRE. ON A1 4 MILES (6KM) S OF WETHERBY.
TEL: 01937 844265

▶ Bramham Park is a rare example of a fine Queen Anne mansion with grand views. The privately owned house was built by Robert Benson during the first half of the 18th century and contains fine furniture, pictures and porcelain. Set in magnificent grounds with ornamental ponds and cascades, it is known as a miniature Versailles. The park is the setting for international horse trials in the summer.

BRAMHAM PARK–BURTON AGNES HALL

Bramham Park, built in the Italianate style by Robert Benson

Gardens open Etr, May Day & Spring BH weekends; House & Gardens open some afternoons Jun–Sep.

▶ A traditional family seaside resort with a harbour, cliff walks around Flamborough Head, coastal wildlife and sandy beaches. There are the usual resort attractions on the seafront and many watersports activities and events. Sewerby Hall, an early 18th-century house, contains a room dedicated to Amy Johnson, the aviation pioneer. The Harbour Museum and Aquarium tells the history of Bridlington Harbour.

▶ Sewerby Hall and Gardens, set in 50 acres (20ha) of parkland overlooking Bridlington Bay, dates back to 1715. The Georgian house, with its 19th-century orangery, contains art galleries, archaeological displays, and an Amy Johnson Room with a collection of her trophies and mementoes. The grounds include magnificent walled Old English and rose gardens and host many events throughout the year, including medieval jousting, a horse pageant and classic cars. Activities for all the family include a children's zoo and play areas, golf, putting, bowls, plus woodland and clifftop walks.

Gardens & zoo open all year daily; Hall open Mar–Apr & Oct–Dec, most days; May–Sep, daily.

▶ Built in 1598, this is a magnificent Elizabethan house, with furniture, pictures and china amassed by the family owners over four centuries. The courtyard between the imposing gatehouse and the hall is formally laid out as a topiary garden. There is a walled garden with a maze, herbaceous borders, clematis, campunala and geranium collections, a jungle garden and woodland walks. The ghost of a young girl is said to haunt the property.

Open Apr–Oct, daily.

BRIDLINGTON
EAST RIDING OF YORKSHIRE.
TOWN ON A165, 10 MILES (16KM) SE OF FILEY

Sewerby Hall & Gardens
TEL: 01262 673769 (PARK) 677874 (HALL)

BURTON AGNES HALL
EAST RIDING OF YORKSHIRE.
HOUSE ON A166, 5 MILES (8KM) SW OF BRIDLINGTON
TEL: 01262 490324

BURTON AGNES HALL—CONISBROUGH CASTLE

Norman Manor House

▶ This is the manor house that Burton Agnes Hall replaced. It is a rare survivor from Norman times, and though later encased in brick it still has its Norman piers and the groined roof of a lower chamber. An upper room and an old donkey wheel can also be seen. The manor house is in the care of English Heritage.

Open all year.

BURTON CONSTABLE HALL
EAST RIDING OF YORKSHIRE.
BURTON CONSTABLE, 1½ MILES (2.5KM) N OF SPROATLEY
TEL: 01964 562400

▶ This superb Elizabethan house was built in 1570, but much of the interior was remodelled in the 18th century. There are magnificent reception rooms and a Tudor long gallery with a pendant roof. The contents range from pictures and furniture (much of it by Thomas Chippendale) to a unique collection of 18th-century scientific instruments. The 200 acres (81ha) of parkland, landscaped by 'Capability' Brown, have oaks, chestnuts and a lake with an island.

Open Etr–Sep, most afternoons.

CLAPHAM
NORTH YORKSHIRE. VILLAGE OFF A65, 6 MILES (10KM) NW OF SETTLE

▶ Clapham, a popular centre for the Three Peaks region (Ingleborough, Pen-y-ghent and Whernside) is one of the prettiest villages in the Dales. The stream which runs through its centre is crossed by old stone bridges and stone cottages line the narrow lanes. Reginald Farrer (1881–1920), from a local family, became a celebrated botanist specialising in alpine species; a local nature trail commemorates his work. The trail leads to Ingleborough Cave where visitors can take a guided tour into a network of caves below Ingleborough.

Yorkshire Dales National Park Centre
TEL: 015242 51419

▶ This is a comprehensive information centre with displays on the local countryside and limestone scenery. A wide range of maps, guides, information leaflets, gifts and souvenirs are stocked and an audio-visual presentation on limestone scenery is available.

Open Apr–Oct, daily. Limited opening Nov–Mar.

CONISBROUGH CASTLE
SOUTH YORKSHIRE. NE OF TOWN CENTRE OFF A630, 5 MILES (8KM) SW OF DONCASTER
TEL: 01709 863329

▶ In the early-12th century, Geoffrey, the young Count of Anjou, plucked a sprig of gorse – *planta genista* – and wore it as a badge in his helmet. What began as a joke ended as a habit, earning the name 'Plantagenet' not only for himself, but also for the ruling dynasty which he founded. He married Matilda, the arrogant, embittered daughter of Henry I, and had a number of children, one of whom would later become Henry II – the first Plantagenet king of England.

Geoffrey was several years younger than his wife, and their marriage was far from happy. Like many medieval barons, he had children from other liaisons, and it was one such illegitimate child, Hamelin Plantagenet, who was resposible for building the unusually shaped tower at Conisbrough.

CONISBROUGH CASTLE—COXWOLD

Hamelin began his building around 1174, and some 15 years later the keep, surrounded by walls with towers, was completed. The walls are 35 feet (11m) tall and 7 feet (2m) thick. The tower is basically round, but with six projecting buttresses, one of which houses a six-sided chapel and some comfortable accommodation. The immensely thick walls of the 95-foot (29m) high tower contain staircases, latrines, fireplaces and hand basins. Despite this economical use of the thick walls, visitors will notice that there are very few windows or arrow loops in the tower. The castle is in the care of English Heritage.

Open all year daily. Closed 24–26 Dec & 1 Jan.

▶ Set at the end of the Howardian Hills, the village's main street is steep and wide, with broad cobbled paving, grassy banks and trees between its mellow houses. The almshouses were built in 1662 by Mary, daughter of Oliver Cromwell and wife of Thomas, Earl of Fauconberg, commemorated by the Fauconberg Arms further up the hill. Mary is said to have buried her father's headless body in nearby Newburgh Priory in a brick vault which has never been opened. It was here that Laurence Sterne, author of *The Life and Opinions of Tristram Shandy, Gentleman* and *A Sentimental Journey through France and Italy*, was parson for eight years, from 1760 until his death. He lived in a house near the church, naming it Shandy Hall. The house is open to the public, and stuffed with memorabilia.

▶ The abbey (English Heritage) was built for the Cistercians and is now a ruin, but enough still stands to show how beautiful it must have been. The ruins date back to the 12th and 13th centuries, and include well-preserved glazed floor tiles still in their original setting. Carved stones and other finds are displayed.

Open end Mar–Oct, daily.

Conisbrough Castle enjoys wonderful views across the surrounding industrial landscape

CLEVELAND HILLS
The distinctive summits of the Cleveland Hills, like Roseberry Topping, escaped the effects of ice pressing round their slopes during various Ice Ages to give them the shape seen today. Beacons warned of the Armada from Roseberry Topping and celebrated the coronation of Queen Elizabeth II. The long-distance footpath, Cleveland Way, runs alongside the hills.

COXWOLD
NORTH YORKSHIRE. VILLAGE OFF A19, 5 MILES (8KM) N OF EASINGWOLD

Byland Abbey
2 MILES (3KM) S OF A170 BETWEEN THIRSK AND HELMSLEY, NEAR COXWOLD VILLAGE
TEL: 01347 868614

DANBY–DEWSBURY

DANBY
NORTH YORKSHIRE. VILLAGE OFF A171, 12 MILES (19KM) W OF WHITBY

Moors Centre
LODGE LN
TEL: 01287 660654

▶ Danby is a typical moors village with a delightful wayside station on the Esk Valley railway, and unspoiled inns and pleasant cafés. The Moors Centre at Danby Lodge is the North York Moors National Park authority's major visitor centre.

▶ The former shooting lodge provides information on the North York Moors National Park, with an exhibition, video, bookshop and information desk. There are riverside and woodland grounds, with terraced gardens, a children's play area and a brass-rubbing centre. Special events are held in summer.
Open all year, Apr–Oct, daily; Nov–Mar, weekends only.

DEWSBURY
WEST YORKSHIRE. TOWN ON A638, 8 MILES (13KM) SW OF LEEDS

Dewsbury town centre

▶ The town was the capital of the 'Heavy Woollen District' of North Kirklees, where methods for reprocessing cloth, to make blankets, work clothes and uniforms, were pioneered in the early-19th century. The Dewsbury Museum concentrates on children at work, play and school; Dewsbury market specialises in textiles. The town centre is a designated conservation area.

DONCASTER–EGTON/EGTON BRIDGE

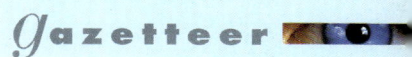

▸ A busy market town on the River Don, Doncaster has seen many recent changes in its community as it witnessed the decline of South Yorkshire's mining industry. However, it commands an excellent position as a principal town on the Great North Road, the Roman route from London, and this advantage has always served the town well. The Romans established a fort here called *Danum*; later Doncaster became an important trading centre in the Middle Ages and a major coaching town during the 18th century.

DONCASTER
SOUTH YORKSHIRE. TOWN OFF A1(M), 17 MILES (27KM) NE OF SHEFFIELD

▸ Brodsworth Hall (English Heritage) is a remarkable example of a Victorian country house which has survived largely intact. The faded grandeur of the family rooms contrast with the well-organised, if spartan, servant's wing. The Victorian gardens are in perfect proportion to the house.
  Open end Apr–Nov, some afternoons.

Brodsworth Hall
BRODSWORTH. BETWEEN THE A635 AND A638
TEL: 01302 722598

▸ The wide-ranging collections include fine and decorative art and sculpture. There are also ceramics, glass and silver, and displays on history, archaeology and natural history. The historical collection of the Kings Own Yorkshire Infantry is housed here.
  Open all year, daily. Closed Good Fri, 25–26 Dec & 1 Jan.

Doncaster Museum & Art Gallery
CHEQUER RD. OFF INNER RING ROAD
TEL: 01302 734293

▸ A monument to Captain Cook, erected in 1827 by Robert Campion, a Whitby banker, is situated on Easby Moor. It is also on the Cleveland Way, and there are views over to Great Ayton were James Cook spent his formative years. Set beside the River Swale, Premonstratensian Easby Abbey (English Heritage) was founded in 1155. Remains of the monks' domestic buildings can be seen.

EASBY
NORTH YORKSHIRE. HAMLET OFF A173, 2 MILES (3KM) SE OF GREAT AYTON

▸ This is a quiet estate village, once an important market place situated between the abbeys of Jervaulx and Middleham. The present village, with pairs of houses facing each other across a wide green, was built by the Earl of Ailesbury in 1809. On the green is a stone dated 1839 with a tap set in it – this was the village's water source.

EAST WITTON
NORTH YORKSHIRE. VILLAGE ON A6108, 2 MILES (3KM) SE OF MIDDLEHAM

▸ These exposed and windswept villages on the North York Moors are separated by the River Esk. Egton Bridge claims to grow the finest gooseberries in the world and an annual Gooseberry Show, now over 200 years old, is held in August. The massive Catholic Church of St Edda, built in 1866, overshadows the village of Egton. Egton Bridge is popular with ramblers who alight at the stop here on the Middlesbrough to Whitby railway line and walk along the Esk Valley to Lealholm to catch the next train.

EGTON/EGTON BRIDGE
NORTH YORKSHIRE. VILLAGES OFF A171, 6 MILES (10KM) SW OF WHITBY

FAIRBURN RSPB NATURE RESERVE—GOMERSAL

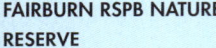
Giggleswick parish church

FAIRBURN RSPB NATURE RESERVE
NORTH YORKSHIRE.
2 SPRINGHOLME CAUDLE HILL.
W OF A1, N OF FERRYBRIDGE
Tel: 01767 680551

FLAMBOROUGH
EAST RIDING OF YORKSHIRE.
VILLAGE ON B1255, 4 MILES
(6KM) NE OF BRIDLINGTON

GIGGLESWICK
NORTH YORKSHIRE. VILLAGE OFF
A65, IMMEDIATELY W OF SETTLE

GOATHLAND
NORTH YORKSHIRE. VILLAGE OFF
A169, 7 MILES (11KM) SW
OF WHITBY

GOMERSAL
WEST YORKSHIRE. VILLAGE ON
A651, 1 MILE (1.5KM) NE OF
CLECKHEATON

▶ One-third of the 618-acre (250ha) RSPB reserve is open water, and over 260 species of bird have been recorded. A visitor centre provides information, and there is an elevated boardwalk, suitable for visitors with disabilities.
  Access to the reserve from the village at all times. Visitor Centre only open Sat, Sun & BHs. Closed 25–26 Dec. Car park and walkway at centre open daily.

▶ Mentioned in the Domesday Book, the village retains a small fishing fleet. Local schoolchildren still dance the traditional Flamborough 'sword dance', using wooden swords. There are steep cliffs at Flamborough Head; the first lighthouse was built here in the 17th century and the present one dates from 1806.

▶ This village, which faces Settle across the River Ribble, retains an old and gentle charm. Many of the buildings date from the 17th century. Rising above the village is Giggleswick Scar, a limestone formation which forms part of the Craven Fault. Just outside the village is the famous Ebbing and Flowing Well.

▶ This picturesque village, high up in the North Yorkshire Moors, has superb examples of stone-built houses. Nearby Mallyan Spout is one of the many waterfalls in the area and just above the village is Moss Swang, a deep and streamless canyon. The North Yorkshire Moors Steam Railway passes through the village.

▶ Gomersal was mentioned in the Domesday Book, when it was owned by Ilbert de Laci. The Methodist church, built in 1827, was known locally as the 'Pork Pie' chapel because of its semi-circular frontage. Charlotte Brontë and John Wesley visited the village, both staying with the Taylor family at Red House.

GOMERSAL–GRASSINGTON

▶ This is a delightful period house decorated as the 1830s home of a Yorkshire wool clothier and merchant. Charlotte Brontë was a frequent visitor here in the 183Cs and the house featured in her novel *Shirley*. Open all year, daily.

▶ The Woggins, Jakey, Jacob's Fold and Chamber End Fold – a village with names like these can only be appealing. Indeed, well before the Romans were mining for lead here, Iron-Age man had been attracted to the area. In Lea Green, hut circles, Celtic lynchets and dewponds are evidence of the 600-year stay of the Brigantes tribe who were to fight the invading Romans. The euphonious 'folds' that run off the

Red House
OXFORD RD. ON A651
Tel: 01274 335100

GRASSINGTON
NORTH YORKSHIRE. VILLAGE ON B6265, 8 MILES (13KM) N OF SKIPTON

Linton Falls near Grassington

gazetteer

GRASSINGTON

THE YORKSHIRE WOLDS
This hill range, which extends from Flamborough Head to the Humber estuary, is a landscape of rolling hills and dales lying mainly between 400 feet (122m) and 600 feet (183m), with the highest point at Garrowby Top. Arable farmland dominates, and there are scattered villages and grand houses.

National Park Centre
COLVEND, HEBDEN RD
TEL: 01756 752774

Halifax city centre

cobbled square and the main street were originally Anglian croft lands, filled in now with grey limestone cottages. Two medieval 'green ways' crossed in Grassington, and in 1381 a weekly market was established by royal charter. Under James I, around 1600, lead ore was extracted up on the moor behind the village and it was these lead mines that were to bring prosperity in the 18th century to this the capital of Upper Wharfedale.

Grassington's main square is edged with shops, inns and pleasing houses. In the main street and in the passages off it are harmonious groups of old stone houses and cottages, mainly 17th- and 18th-century, some two- and some three-storey, all coming together to make an exceptionally attractive village. Grassington Hall dates partly from the late-13th century, while Theatre Cottage is a barn converted to a theatre early in the 19th century.

▶ The centre is a useful introduction to the Yorkshire Dales National Park. It has a video and a display on 'Wharfedale – Gateway to the Park', and maps, guides and local information are available. There is also a 24-hour public access information service through computer screens and a full tourist information service.

Open Apr–Oct, daily; some weekends Nov–Mar.

GREAT DRIFFIELD—HALIFAX

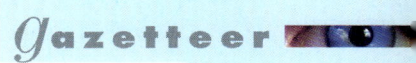gazetteer

▸ This agricultural town is known as the 'Capital of the Wolds'. The oldest part of the town is Moot Hill which was the meeting place of the Saxon 'Town Moot'. An annual agricultural show has been held here since 1854 and there is a cattle market on Thursdays. The Driffield Canal was opened in 1772.

▸ The stone-built town is centred around an old village green with a market cross and stocks. Old stone terraces with cobbled streets remain and there is also more modern housing. Patrick and Maria Brontë were married in St Oswald's Church in 1812. Harry Ramsden's, the most famous fish and chip shop in the world, opened its first restaurant here in 1928.

▸ This attractive village is situated in a delightful wooded valley where the Lowdale Beck meets the River Derwent. Built of mellow, local stone, the estate cottages and houses cluster around the 11th-century Church of St Peter. The old manor house (not open) remains in the village.

▸ Halifax, the main town of Calderdale, rose to prominence during the textile boom of the 18th and 19th centuries. The focal point of the town is Piece Hall, built in 1779 as a market place for the surrounding cottage wool industry.

The subsequent advent of steam power and the Industrial Revolution brought the greatest prosperity to Halifax, which became known as the 'town of 100 trades' because of the many industries that sprang up around the textile industry.

Calderdale Industrial Museum, adjacent to Piece Hall, houses working looms and mill machinery. A 15th-century timber-framed house, just outside the centre, is Shibden Hall which also houses the Folk Museum of West Yorkshire. The interior gives an intimate picture of life in the 17th and 18th centuries and the folk museum depicts life in a 19th-century village.

The town hall was designed by Sir Charles Barry, who also designed the Houses of Parliament in London. Halifax has a large parish church dating from the 12th and 13th centuries, although most of the present building is from the 15th century.

▸ Built by Edward Akroyd in the 1860s, this Renaissance-style building is set in parkland on a hill overlooking the town. It has an outstanding collection of costumes and textiles from many periods and parts of the world, including a new gallery featuring East European textiles. There is also a section on toys, and the museum of the Duke of Wellington's Regiment is housed here. Temporary exhibitions are held and there is a

GREAT DRIFFIELD
EAST RIDING OF YORKSHIRE. TOWN OFF A166, 11 MILES (18KM) SW OF BRIDLINGTON

GUISELEY
WEST YORKSHIRE. TOWN ON A65, 10 MILES (16KM) NW OF LEEDS

HACKNESS
NORTH YORKSHIRE. VILLAGE OFF A171, 5 MILES (8KM) W OF SCARBOROUGH

HALIFAX
WEST YORKSHIRE. TOWN ON A58, 7 MILES (11KM) SW OF BRADFORD

Bankfield Museum
AKROYD PARK, BOOTHTOWN RD
TEL: 01422 354823 & 352334

HALIFAX

Calderdale Industrial Museum
CENTRAL WORKS, SQUARE RD
TEL: 01422 358087

▶ Working machines representing 100 years of local industry, from textiles to toffee wrapping and steam engines to washing machines, can be seen here, with all the sounds and smells to match. There is an activity area for children under six called the Workplays and also a lively programme of events, activities and workshops.

Open all year, most days. Closed Xmas and 1 Jan.

Open all year, most days. Closed Mon (ex BH), 25–26 Dec & 1 Jan.

Eureka! The Museum for Children
DISCOVERY RD. M62 EXIT 24
FOLLOW BROWN TOURIST
INFORMATION SIGNS TO HALIFAX
CENTRE (A629)
TEL: 01422 330069

▶ Eureka! is the first 'hands-on' museum in Britain designed especially for children up to the age of 12. Wherever you go in Eureka! you can touch, listen and smell, as well as look. There are four main exhibition areas – Me and My Body, Living and Working Together, Invent, Create, Communicate and Things – where visitors can find out how the human body and senses work, investigate the design and uses of everyday objects, role-play in the buildings around the Town Square and explore the world of communications from basic forms through to the high-tech inventions of today. Outside in the park you can exercise on the Health Trail and enter the Hazard Dome, an audio-visual presentation with special 3-D effects about home safety. An extensive programme of exhibitions, activities, workshops and performances runs throughout the year.

Open all year, daily. Closed 24–26 Dec.

Piece Hall
TEL: 01422 358087

▶ The merchants of Halifax built this elegant and unique hall in 1779 as a trading place for pieces of cloth. It has over 300 merchants' rooms around a courtyard and now houses an industrial museum, art galleries and shops selling antiques, books and other specialities. An open market is held on Friday and Saturday, and a flea market on Thursday. There is a Tourist Information Centre, free entertainment most weekends, and a series of exhibitions, workshops, activities and events are held during the year.

Open all year, daily. Closed 25–26 Dec. Industrial Museum and Art Gallery, open most days.

Shibden Hall
LISTER'S RD
TEL: 01422 352246 &
321455

▶ The house dates back to the early-15th century, and its rooms have been laid out to illustrate life in different periods of its history. The vast 17th-century barn has a fine collection of horse-drawn vehicles and houses a blacksmith and saddler. Craft weekends feature over 30 craftworkers demonstrating traditional skills. There is a lively programme of craft events, workshops and family activities.

Open Mar–Nov, daily; Feb, Sun afternoons only. Closed Dec–Jan.

HAREWOOD HOUSE & BIRD GARDEN

▶ The home of the Lascelles family for over 200 years, Harewood House is an exquisite example of the work of both John Carr of York, the original architect, and Robert Adam who was brought in at a later date to design all the interiors. Even the furniture was specially made for the house by Thomas Chippendale, who was born at nearby Otley in the Wharfe Valley. But things have not stood still at Harewood; alterations were made in Victorian times by Sir Charles Barry, architect of the Houses of Parliament. He added a third storey and transformed the south façade with an Italianate terrace.

An ancient family, one of whom came to Britain with William the Conqueror, the Lascelles increased their fortune through their Barbados sugar plantations in the late-17th century, facilitating the building of their new mansion at Harewood. Subsequent generations added the fine art collections – the first Viscount Lascelles amassed the collection of Chinese celadon and French porcelain and commissioned watercolours from the leading artists of the day. The 6th Earl of Harewood put together a splendid collection of Italian paintings, and with his wife, Princess Mary, the Princess Royal, set about the restoration of the house, bringing back some of the character which Robert Adam had intended it should have.

The house has been open to visitors almost since it was built, when interested sightseers were taken around by arrangement with the housekeeper. Today, most of the original building is on show and the family's private apartments are on the top floor. The entrance hall, with its fine plasterwork and classical lines, shows Robert Adam's unity of style to perfection, but today it is dominated by the most important modern work of art in the house – Jacob Epstein's statue of Adam (the biblical one). From here a tour of the house takes in magnificent formal state rooms and such wonderfully welcoming and comfortable rooms as Lord Harewood's sitting room and the lovely old library.

In every one of the rooms is a stunning array of works of art, fine china and beautiful furniture, mingled with family photographs and memorabilia. Beyond the terrace are lovely grounds which include a lake and a famous bird garden.

Open mid Mar–Oct, daily. Grounds and Bird Garden also open weekends Nov–Dec.

HAREWOOD HOUSE & BIRD GARDEN
WEST YORKSHIRE. JUNC A61/A659 LEEDS TO HARROGATE ROAD
TEL: 0113 288 6331

Harewood House is hailed as a showpiece of 18th-century architecture

HARROGATE

HARROGATE
NORTH YORKSHIRE. TOWN ON A61, 13 MILES (21KM) N OF LEEDS

▶ Harrogate evolved as a spa in 1571, ranking among the finest in the world, and as such it quickly became a popular venue among the rich Victorians. A handsome town with dignified Victorian buildings, tree-lined boulevards, gardens and wide open spaces, it has never lost its charm and elegance, typified by Montpellier Parade and Gardens in the centre of the town.

Since the building of the town's International Conference Centre, Harrogate has become well established as a major business centre. Harrogate is also popular with day visitors and with tourists. The Royal Pump Room, now a museum of Harrogate's history, was built in 1842 to enclose the old sulphur well which is still there to this day, and the splendid Turkish baths are still in use at the Royal Baths Assembly Rooms, built in 1897 to house a myriad of water-based treatments. The streets are decorated with ornate cast-iron canopies and floral baskets and lined with old-fashioned shops, tea rooms and restaurants. Harrogate is home to the prestigious Harlow Carr Botanical Gardens.

Harlow Carr Botanical Gardens
CRAG LANE, OTLEY RD. OFF B6162, 1½ MILES (2.5KM) FROM HARROGATE CENTRE
TEL: 01423 565418

▶ The gardens were begun in 1950 on a rough site of pasture and woodland. Today there are 68 acres (28ha) of ornamental and woodland gardens, including the trial grounds of the Northern Horticultural Society. There are craft weekends in the summer. Courses, demonstrations and practical workshops are held in the study centre.
Open all year, daily.

The Royal Pump Room Museum
ROYAL PDE
TEL: 01423 503340

▶ The octagonal Pump Room building holds changing exhibitions from the museum's own collections. This part of the building still houses the original sulphur wells, now below modern street level. The wells are enclosed by glass to contain their pungent smell, but the water can be tasted, by those brave enough, at the original spa counter.
Open all year, daily. Closed 25–26 Dec & 1 Jan.

The old Pump Room stands in Harrogate's town centre

WENSLEYDALE AND THE YORKSHIRE DALES

Cycle ride

*T*he main A684 is the principal east–west route through the Yorkshire Dales National Park, making Wensleydale probably the most accessible of the Dales. But this ride explores both sides of this attractive valley by using quiet side-roads. On the route you can see the highest market town in the country, two of Yorkshire's most famous waterfalls and some of the finest countryside in the Yorkshire Dales.

INFORMATION

Total Distance
25 miles (40km)

Grade
Easy

OS Map
Outdoor Leisure 1:25,000 sheet 30 (Yorkshire Dales, Northern & Central areas.)

Tourist Information
Hawes, tel: 01969 667450
Aysgarth Falls, tel: 01969 663424

Cycle Shops/Hire
Ian Rawlins, Askrigg, tel: 01969 650455

Refreshments
There are plenty of pubs and tea rooms along the route – in Hawes, Askrigg, Carperby, Aysgarth and Bainbridge – and a café in the National Park Centre at Aysgarth Falls. Semer Water makes a good picnic site.

START

The little market town of Hawes lies on the A684 in the heart of the Yorkshire Dales, north-west of Ripon. There is a free car park in the town, plus pay-and-display parking at the Dales Countryside Museum.

DIRECTIONS

1. Leave Hawes travelling westwards along the A684, towards Sedbergh and Kirkbymoorside. It is just a mile

Winter snow lies on the hills of Wensleydale above Hawes

Cycle ride

WENSLEYDALE AND THE YORKSHIRE DALES

(1.5km) to the little hamlet of Appersett. Cross two bridges – spanning first Widdale Beck, followed by the River Ure – before bearing sharp right, signed 'Hardraw and Askrigg'.

2. After a mile (1.5km) you arrive in the village of Hardraw. Make sure to visit Hardraw Force, a spectacular waterfall; entry is through the Green Dragon pub. Continue along the road towards Askrigg (ignoring turn-offs left and right, to Muker and Hawes). The road is level, through the enticing landscape of this gently sloping U-shaped valley. Wensleydale's river – the Ure – is visible at most points during the ride. Half a mile (1km) beyond a turn-off to Bainbridge, you reach the village of Askrigg.

3. The road winds up through this compact village, best known today as a Herriot 'film set', although well worth exploring in its own right. Leaving the village, your route is signed 'Carperby and Leyburn'. A steep climb is followed by level riding, through a typical Dales landscape of dry-stone walls, field barns and scattered farmsteads. Just before the village of Carperby, go right, signed 'Aysgarth Falls'.

4. To investigate the trio of waterfalls (on foot) turn right after ½ mile (1km), immediately beyond a railway bridge, into the Aysgarth Falls National Park

Centre. Afterwards, continue steeply down the road, cross the bridge over the River Ure, and climb (or walk) very steeply uphill to meet the A684 at a T-junction. Go right, towards Aysgarth, Bainbridge and Hawes. After ½ mile (1km) you will pass through the village of Aysgarth.

Leave the village, turn left, signed 'Thornton Rust'. The roads climbs steadily to give panoramic views across Wensleydale.

5. After 2 miles (3km) of level riding you reach the characterful cottages of 'Thornton Rust'. A further 2 miles (3km) brings you to the hamlet of Cubeck; freewheel downhill to meet the A684 once again, at Worton. Go left, signed 'Bainbridge and Hawes'. Just before the road descends into Bainbridge (a lovely village whose green is as big as a meadow), bear left on a road signed to Semer Water and Stalling Busk. Climb uphill,

Hardraw Force plummets into a natural amphitheatre

keeping right when the road forks, to arrive at an almost Lakeland scene: Semer Water in the valley bottom hemmed in by hills. Keep right at the next fork, overlooking the lake (ignore a sign to Stalling Busk), and ride down to the lake.

6. Cross a handsome three-arched bridge over the River Bain, and negotiate a 1-in-4 hill up to a T-junction. Go right, and immediately left, signed 'Burtersett and Hawes'.

A steep climb is followed by a long descent (crossing the old Roman road from Bainbridge to Ilkley) to arrive in Burtersett village. Continue downhill to rejoin the A684 for the last time; bear left to cycle the last mile (1.5km) back into Hawes to complete the tour and for some well-earned refreshment.

WENSLEYDALE AND THE YORKSHIRE DALES

Cycle ride

PLACES OF INTEREST

Hawes

The 'capital' of Upper Wensleydale, Hawes is a busy little town – especially on Tuesday, market day. The Dales Countryside Museum, occupying the old Hawes railway station, displays tools, bygones and curios that help to show what life was like in earlier times in the Yorkshire Dales.

(See also page 30.)

Hardraw Force

Hardraw Force crashes over the lip of a limestone crag into a pool 90 feet (27m) below. It is England's highest waterfall and a spectacular sight – especially after heavy rain. Entry is via the Green Dragon pub (small fee payable) and the walk to the waterfall takes only a few minutes. An old tradition of holding brass-band contests there has been revived; they take place every September.

Askrigg

Until Hawes took on the mantle, Askrigg was the main market town of the upper valley; now only the stepped market cross remains. The village has featured in James Herriot's *All Creatures Great and Small*, the long-running television series written by Yorkshire vet, James Alfred Whight. Viewers will recognise Cringley House as the vets' home 'Skelgate House', and also the King's Arms pub opposite, which became the 'Drovers Arms'.

Aysgarth Falls

The waterfalls at Aysgarth have been much-loved landmarks as long as visitors have come to the Dales. The usually placid River Ure hammers over rocks in a series of three splendid falls, best viewed from a footpath at the visitor centre.

(See also page 6.)

Semer Water

Nestling in the little side valley of Raydale, Semer Water is one of the few areas of open water in the national park. It drains into the River Ure at Bainbridge via the River Bain – reckoned, at 3 miles (5km), to be the shortest river in the country.

Legend has it that there is a lost village beneath Semer Water; at night a phantom church bell has been heard to toll.

WHAT TO LOOK OUT FOR

Most of the Dales (Swaledale, Wharfedale, Airedale etc) are named after the rivers that run through them. Wensleydale is an exception, taking its name from Wensley, a village further down the dale. The river is the Ure, and 'Yoredale' is an old name for the valley. There are many opportunities on this ride to stop by the riverside, for rest and refreshment. Look out for typical waterside birds, such as the dipper, yellow wagtail and the huge grey heron.

Windsurfers skim across Semer Water

HAWES—HAWORTH

The thriving market town of Hawes is an ideal place to buy local produce

HAWES
NORTH YORKSHIRE. SMALL TOWN ON A684, 14 MILES (22KM) SE OF KIRKBY STEPHEN

Dales Countryside Museum Centre
STATION YARD
TEL: 01969 667450

HAWORTH
WEST YORKSHIRE. TOWN OFF A629, 2 MILES (3KM) SW OF KEIGHLEY

▶ Situated in Upper Wensleydale on the River Ure, Hawes is the main centre for the northern part of the Yorkshire Dales National Park. This is a farming area; local produce is sold at the busy Tuesday market and the Leyburn Road is where farmers sell their livestock. The famous Wensleydale cheese is made locally at the Wensleydale Creamery which has a museum, a flourishing visitor centre, shop and viewing platforms into the works.

(See also Cycle ride: Wensleydale and the Yorkshire Dales, page 27.)

▶ The Dales Countryside Museum contains displays and an extensive collection of bygones and farming implements which explain the changing landscapes and communities of the area. There is a full national park and tourist information service, including 24-hour public information terminals, maps, guides, publications and souvenirs.

Open Apr–Oct, daily. Limited winter opening.

▶ Haworth is an industrial Pennine village of steep streets and dark stone weavers' cottages. But the industry that is its lifeblood now is not textiles, but the Brontës. For it was in the parsonage here that from 1820 to 1861 the talented Brontë sisters, Charlotte, Emily and Anne lived with their wayward brother Branwell and their father, writing their intensely romantic and powerful novels, including *Jane Eyre* and *Wuthering Heights*. The rapid expansion of the weaving trade in the 18th century had left Haworth's twisted streets cramped with tall terraces of weavers' houses, so grim and grimy and riddled with

HAWORTH

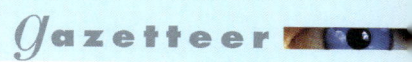

disease as to horrify Maria Brontë when she arrived with her husband, Reverend Patrick Brontë, and their six children. Two of the children died in childhood, and Maria herself died only a year after moving here. Pilgrims making their devotional way today to the shrine of the Brontë Parsonage Museum toil up the cobbled street that is still the heart of Haworth, above the mills and housing estates in the valley bottom. Resisting if they can the lure of countless cafés and souvenir shops, they reach The Black Bull, one of Branwell's drinking holes, and then the church with its family vault and finally the Parsonage, an 18th-century sandstone building poignantly furnished as it was in the Brontës' day. Beyond are the windswept moors.

▶ The house contains personal memorabilia, including the furniture Charlotte bought with the proceeds of her literary success, her dress, bonnet and tiny shoes, along with the Brontë children's earliest literary efforts and their handmade 'little books'. The Brontë Society cares for the parsonage, which opened as a museum in 1928.

Open all year daily. Closed mid Jan–1st week Feb & 24–27 Dec.

▶ The line was built mainly to serve the valley's mills, and goes through the heart of Brontë country. It begins at Keighley (also a main line station), and then climbs up to Haworth, the railway workshops and headquarters. The terminus is at Oxenhope, which has a museum and restoration building. There are approximately 36 steam engines and eight diesels. Special events are planned throughout the year.

All year weekend service, but daily all BH weeks & Jul–1st week in Sep.

Brontë Parsonage Museum
ON THE A6033 LEADING FROM A629
TEL: 01535 642323

Keighley & Worth Valley Railway & Museum
KEIGHLEY, HAWORTH, OXENHOPE & INGROW WEST
TEL: 01535 645214 & 677777

Haworth is one of the six stops on the Keighley and Worth Valley Railway

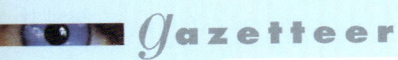

HEBDEN BRIDGE–HELMSLEY

HEBDEN BRIDGE
WEST YORKSHIRE. TOWN ON A646, 7 MILES (11KM) W OF HALIFAX

▶ This ancient mill town, known as the 'capital of the Pennines', has seen much restoration work since 1970. Many of the old mill buildings have been converted into museums and other places of interest; but the typical 'double-decker' houses can still be seen. The Rochdale Canal has also been restored and today offers many leisure facilities. Hardcastle Crags (owned by the National Trust), is a beauty spot to the north-west of Hebden Bridge, which comprises a steep wooded valley and rock outcrops. A network of paths leads through the woods to Hedben Water.

The Hebden Bridge Marina on the Rochdale Canal

HELMSLEY
NORTH YORKSHIRE. SMALL TOWN ON A170, 12 MILES (19KM) E OF THIRSK

▶ This is one of the most popular of Yorkshire's market towns, where attractive old inns, houses and shops surround the market square. The town is overlooked by its ruined medieval castle and by All Saints' Church. Duncombe Park is open to the public; the grounds provide an important habitat for wildlife.

Duncombe Park
1M (1.5KM) FROM TOWN CENTRE, OFF A170
TEL: 01439 770213 & 771115

▶ Duncombe Park stands at the heart of a spectacular 30-acre (12ha) early 18th-century landscape garden which is set in 300 acres (121ha) of dramatic parkland around the River Rye. The house, originally built in 1713, was gutted by fire in 1879 and rebuilt in 1895. Its principal rooms are a fine example of the type of grand interior popular at the turn of the century. Home of the Duncombes for

HELMSLEY—HOLMFIRTH

gazetteer

300 years, for much of this century the house was a girls' school. In 1985 the present Lord and Lady Feversham decided to make it a family home again, and after major restoration opened the house to the public in 1990. Part of the garden and parkland were designated a National Nature Reserve in 1994. Special events are held throughout the year.

Open: House & Gardens, Etr wknd—beginning of Nov, most days; May—Sep, daily.

▶ The ruined castle (English Heritage) dates from the 12th century and later, and stands within enormous earthworks. It was besieged for three months in the Civil War, and destroyed in 1644.

Open all year, Apr—Oct, daily; Nov—mid Mar, certain days. Closed 24—26 Dec & 1 Jan.

▶ The village overlooks Hebden Bridge and the Hardcastle Crags and has become one of the main tourist centres of Calderdale. It is one of only three places in Britain where there are two churches in one churchyard. Every year on Good Friday the 'Paceggers Play' takes place in Weavers Square, telling the story of St George and his heroic deeds.

▶ In this small mill town picturesque groupings of sturdy sandstone cottages, ginnels, and courtyards mix with magnificent textile mills set proudly upon the landscape. Holmfirth is now synonymous with the television series *Last of the Summer Wine*, which is filmed here – look out for Sid's Café and Nora Batty's steps. There is a permanent photographic exhibition of the series.

Helmsley Castle
TEL: *01439 770442*

HEPTONSTALL
WEST YORKSHIRE. VILLAGE OFF A646, 1 MILE (2KM) NW OF HEBDEN BRIDGE

HOLMFIRTH
WEST YORKSHIRE. TOWN ON A635, 5 MILES (8KM) S OF HUDDERSFIELD

Holmfirth, an engaging town built at the confluence of the Holme and the Ribble

HOLE OF HORCUM
This beauty spot lies on the Levisham Moor – a hollow forming a vast natural amphitheatre, which is sometimes known as the Devil's Punchbowl.

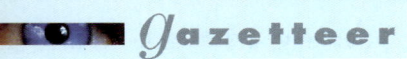

HORNSEA

East Riding of Yorkshire. Small town on B1243, 14 miles (22km) NE of Hull

Hornsea Freeport
Tel: 01964 534211

Hornsea Museum
11 Newbegin
Tel: 01964 533443 & 533430

HUDDERSFIELD

West Yorkshire. Town off M62, 11 miles (18km) S of Bradford

HOWARDIAN HILLS

A limestone hill range covering 77 square miles (199sq km) separating the vales of York and Pickering. There is abundant wildlife and archaeological interest.

Huddersfield Art Gallery
Princess Alexandra Walk
Tel: 01484 221964 ext 1962

▶ This is an attractive seaside town with a fine sandy beach and a long history of smuggling. Hornsea Mere is the largest freshwater lake in Humberside and has a RSPB nature reserve. Hornsea Pottery, as well as selling pottery bargains, also has a leisure park with Butterfly World, birds of prey and a plant centre.

▶ This unique park offers both leisure and retail facilities. Leisure attractions include the Yorkshire Car Collection, Birds of Prey, Model Village, Butterfly World, Neptune's Kingdom, an outdoor adventure playground and guided tours of the pottery. Over 28 famous high street names sell merchandise at reduced prices.
   Open all year, daily. Closed 25–26 Dec.

▶ A former farmhouse and its outbuildings now illustrate local life and history, with 19th-century period rooms and a dairy, craft tools and farming implements. Photographs, industries and local personalities are also featured.
   Open Etr–Sep, daily.

▶ A traditional Yorkshire textile town, Huddersfield has all the hallmarks of Victorian wealth that characterise so many towns in this region. A great Cloth Hall was built in 1766 by the Ramsden family who also brought the Ramsden Canal and the railway to Huddersfield. The Victorian railway station was designed by J P Pritchett in the classical manner with long colonnades. It was completed in 1850 and is considered to be one of the finest railway buildings in England. The town hall was built in 1878, and markets and arcades were built at around the same time.
   In 1920 the Huddersfield Corporation purchased the Ramsden estate, including almost all of the town centre, from Sir J F Ramsden, the 6th Baronet, and the place is often referred to as 'the town that bought itself'.
   The town centre has been improved considerably by pedestrianisation schemes and stone-cleaning of the Victorian buildings. The cast-iron work, glazed walls and elaborate details of Brook Street outdoor market, built in 1887 as a wholesale market, have been restored and it now serves as a general market.

▶ The changing displays from the permanent collection include British oil paintings, watercolours, drawings and sculpture from the mid-19th century onwards. Temporary loan art, craft and photography exhibitions are also held throughout the year.
   Open all year, most days. Closed Sun and BH.

HUDDERSFIELD—HULL gazetteer

▶ Displays on the development of the cloth industry and a collection of horse-drawn vehicles are shown, together with natural history, archaeology, toys and folk exhibits. There is a full programme of events and temporary exhibitions.

Open all year, daily. Closed Xmas.

▶ Hull, officially known as Kingston upon Hull, lies on the southern margin of the plain of Holderness, its port and harbour washed by the tidal flow of the River Humber. Today it is a busy port with much freight and passenger traffic to and from Europe. The Town Docks Museum defines the city's maritime history, which spans 700 years, with galleries on whaling, fishing and shipping.

William Wilberforce, the famous slavery abolitionist, was born in Hull in 1759, and his fine Jacobean house is now a museum commemorating his life and works. Wilberforce was a pupil at the old grammar school, which was built in 1583 – it is now a museum of social history called 'The Story of Hull'.

Many of the oldest parts of Hull were bombed out of existence in World War II, but subsequent building in the town centre has been sensitive. The old town, much of which dates back 800 years, is full of narrow cobbled streets and quays with old taverns. Whitefriargate takes its name from the monastery of the Carmelites or White Friars which once stood on the site. Today it is the main shopping street of the old town. The harbour area is now attractively developed as a

Tolson Memorial Museum
RAVENSKNOWLE PARK. ON A629
TEL: 01484 223830

HULL
EAST RIDING OF YORKSHIRE. CITY ON A63, 50 MILES (80KM) E OF LEEDS

Spurn *lightship, built in 1927, now moored in the marina at Hull*

gazetteer

HULL–HUMBER BRIDGE

marina, and the warehouse buildings have been converted into hotels and apartments. In an imaginative scheme to create a city trail, Hull can be explored by following a series of specially commissioned fish reliefs set into the pavements throughout the centre.

The city is pleasantly free from high-rise blocks, offering clear views of the Humber estuary and the famous Humber Bridge.

Maister House
160 High St
Tel: 01482 324114

▶ The house, rebuilt in the mid-18th century, is noted for its splendid stone and wrought-iron staircase, ornate stucco work and finely carved doors. Only the staircase and entrance hall are open. Maister House is in the care of the National Trust.

Open all year, most days.

'Streetlife' – Hull Museum of Transport
High Street
Tel: 01482 613902

▶ This purpose-built museum uses a 'hands-on' approach to trace 200 years of transport history. With a vehicle collection of national importance, state-of-the-art animatronic displays and stunningly authentic scenarios, you are swept back in time to Hull's Old Town which has been brought vividly to life.

Open all year, daily. Closed 24–25 Dec & Good Fri.

Town Docks Museum
Queen Victoria Square
Tel: 01482 613902

▶ Hull's maritime history is illustrated here, with displays on whales and whaling, ships and shipping, and other aspects of this Humber port. There is also a Victorian court room which is used for temporary exhibitions. The restored dock area, with its fine Victorian and Georgian buildings, is well worth exploring too.

Open all year, daily. Closed 25–26 Dec, 1 Jan & Good Fri.

Wilberforce House
23–25 High St
Tel: 01482 613902

▶ The early 17th-century merchants' house was the birthplace of William Wilberforce, who went on to become a leading campaigner against slavery. There are Jacobean and Georgian rooms and displays on Wilberforce, the anti-slavery campaign, silver, costumes, historic room settings, decorative art and dolls. The house also has secluded gardens. There is a special exhibition, The A–Z of Costume, with displays of Hull Museum's extensive costume collection.

Open all year, daily. Closed 25–26 Dec, 1 Jan & Good Fri.

HUMBER BRIDGE
East Riding of Yorkshire.
Bridge carrying A15 across the Humber between Hessle and Barton-upon-Humber

▶ Sweeping over the flat landscape and the rolling waters of the estuary for over 1¼ miles (2km) the graceful suspension bridge was designed by the London engineering firm of Freeman, Fox and Partners. It took eight years to complete, and when it was opened by the Queen in 1981, its single central span was the longest in the world at 4,626 feet (1,410m). The structure contains 470,000 tons of concrete, and its twin 533-feet (152m) towers support massive cables in which there

HUMBER BRIDGE–ILKLEY

gazetteer

are altogether 44,000 miles (70,700km) of wire – enough to go round the world one and a half times. The four-laned road deck is almost 100 feet (30m) above the water at high tide and there are pedestrian and cycle paths on either side. There is a spectacular view of the bridge from a special parking area off the A15 on the south side of the river, and another parking area on the north side. The Humber is not really a river, but the estuary of the Yorkshire Ouse and the River Trent, which drain a vast area of 9,550 square miles (24,750sq km). One of the major trade arteries in the country, it is close to a mile (1.5km) wide at the confluence of the two rivers, and a deepwater channel runs 22 miles (35km) from Hull to the mouth at the North Sea, where the Humber is more than 7 miles (11km) wide.

▶ This is a beautiful village lying in the small valley of Hutton Beck. The traditional stone cottages, with pantiled roofs, are built around a large green. The main attraction, however, is the Ryedale Folk Museum a fascinating open-air collection which includes a reconstructed medieval thatched cruck house as well as an ancient glassworks, a blacksmith's shop and displays of local crafts.

HUTTON-LE-HOLE
NORTH YORKSHIRE. VILLAGE OFF A170, 2 MILES (3KM) N OF KIRKBYMOORSIDE

▶ Ilkley, a well-known spa town on the River Wharfe surrounded by fine moorland scenery, became a fashionable commuter town with the coming of the railway line between Leeds and Bradford in the 1860s and with the Yorkshire woollen industry.

Originally an Iron-Age setttlement, it was subsequently occupied by the Romans who built a camp here to protect their crossing of the river.

ILKLEY
WEST YORKSHIRE. TOWN ON A65, 10 MILES (16KM) N OF BRADFORD

The packhorse bridge at Ilkley

37

gazetteer

ILKLEY—KEIGHLEY

They named the town that sprang up *Olicana*, which, with the familiar 'ley' (Anglo-Saxon for pasture) added, gave rise to its existing name. All Saints' Church has three Anglo-Saxon crosses in the churchyard and behind is a grassy mound where a little fort was built. In the town's museum are altars carved in gritstone, dedicated to the Roman gods.

The most famous local attraction is Ilkley Moor, which has been immortalised in the well-known song. The spring at White Wells on Ilkley Moor brought visitors to the town in the 18th century, and a small bathhouse was built where elderly patients were encouraged to take a dip in the healing waters of the 'heather spa', as it was known.

Manor House Gallery & Museum
CASTLE YARD, CHURCH ST.
BEHIND ILKLEY PARISH CHURCH,
ON A65
TEL: 01943 600066

▶ The Elizabethan manor house is one of Ilkley's few buildings to pre-date the 19th century. The house was built on the site of a Roman fort and part of the Roman wall can be seen, together with Roman relics and displays on archaeology. Inside there is also a collection of 17th- and 18th-century farmhouse parlour and kitchen furniture, while the art gallery exhibits works by contemporary artists and craftsmen.

Open all year, most days. Closed Good Fri, 25–28 Dec.

INGLETON
NORTH YORKSHIRE. VILLAGE ON
B6255, 6 MILES (10KM) SE
OF KIRKBY LONSDALE

▶ The village is the gateway to the Three Peaks of Ingleborough, Whernside and Pen-y-ghent. Steep, winding streets lead down to the gorge and the famous waterfalls which were discovered by Joseph Carr in 1865. It was not until 1885 that they were made accessible to the general public.

KEIGHLEY
WEST YORKSHIRE. TOWN ON
A629, 9 MILES (14KM) NW
OF BRADFORD

▶ This busy market and textile town has fine examples of Victorian and Edwardian architecture along with modern buildings. Many of the cobbled side-streets remain. The Keighley and Worth Valley Railway (see Haworth, page 31) runs regular services, with steam trains in the

A variety of locomotives steam along the thriving Keighley and Worth Valley Railway line

summer months, and has been used in films such as *The Railway Children* and *Yanks*.

▶ French furniture from London's Victoria and Albert Museum is displayed, together with collections of local and natural history, ceramics, dolls, geological items and minerals. The grounds of this 19th-century mansion contain a play area and an aviary.
   Open all year, most days. Closed Good Fri, 25–28 Dec.

▶ This charming 17th-century manor house (National Trust) is typical of its kind, although the plasterwork and oak panelling are contemporary. A small secluded garden is situated in the grounds, which also features one of the largest medieval tithe barns in the north of England.
   Open Apr–Oct, most days.

▶ The village overlooks large parts of the vales of York and Mowbray. The Kilburn White Horse, carved into the turf in 1857, was the brainchild of Thomas Taylor. Today it is maintained by a committee of local people. Kilburn was also the home of Robert Thompson, the 'Mouseman', a wood carver and cabinet-maker who made some furniture for the local church. Thompson specialised in ecclesiastical furniture; he made pews and pulpits for many churches in Yorkshire and examples of his work can be found in York Minster and London's Westminster Abbey. Robert Thompson's signature, a small carved mouse, can be found on all his work. His workshops and showrooms are open to the public.

▶ This ancient fell village is overlooked by the huge limestone Kilnsey Crag, which dominates the landscape for miles around. Kilnsey Park Centre is devoted to rural life. Attractions include ducks and fish, and there are displays of local crafts.

▶ The village is home to the Flamingo Land Theme Park and Zoo which is set in the grounds of the old Hall. Over 100 attractions include white-knuckle rides, children's rides, entertainment shows, a circus, an extensive zoo and a bird walk.

▶ Set on an entrancing site on the banks of the River Derwent, the ruins of this former house of Augustinian canons dominate the quiet village of Kirkham. The remains of the finely sculptured 13th-century gatehouse and lavatorium, where the monks washed in leaded troughs, are now in the care of English Heritage.
   Open Apr–Sep, daily, afternoons only.

Cliffe Castle Museum & Gallery
SPRING GARDENS LN. NW OF TOWN OFF A629
TEL: 01535 618230

East Riddlesden Hall
BRADFORD RD. 1M (1.5KM) NE OF KEIGHLEY ON SOUTH SIDE OF BRADFORD RD.
TEL: 01535 607075

KILBURN
NORTH YORKSHIRE
VILLAGE OFF A170, 6 MILES (10KM) E OF THIRSK

KILNSEY
NORTH YORKSHIRE. HAMLET ON B6160, 3 MILES (5KM) NW OF GRASSINGTON

KIRBY MISPERTON
NORTH YORKSHIRE. VILLAGE OFF A169, 3 MILES (5KM) S OF PICKERING

KIRKHAM PRIORY
NORTH YORKSHIRE. PRIORY 5 MILES (8KM) SW OF MALTON ON MINOR ROAD OFF A64
TEL: 01653 618768

gazetteer

KNARESBOROUGH–LASTINGHAM

KNARESBOROUGH

NORTH YORKSHIRE. TOWN ON A59, 3 MILES (5KM) NE OF HARROGATE

Knaresborough Castle
TEL: 01423 503340

The remains of Knaresborough Castle, above

LASTINGHAM

NORTH YORKSHIRE. VILLAGE OFF A170, 6 MILES (10KM) NW OF PICKERING

▶ This is a picturesque market town, perched precariously high over the River Nidd, with Georgian houses, narrow streets, a maze of alleys, boating and pleasant riverside walks. Curious attractions include the ruins of a 12th-century castle, England's oldest chemist's shop and the legendary Mother Shipton's Cave with its Petrifying Well.

▶ High above the town of Knaresborough, the ruins of this 14th-century castle look down over the gorge of the River Nidd. This imposing fortress was once the hiding place of Thomas à Becket's murderers and it also served as a prison for Richard II. Remains include the keep, the sally-port, parts of the curtain wall and the old court of Knaresborough, part of which also dates from the 14th century. It now houses a local history museum, and entrance is part of the combined ticket price. A gallery is devoted to the Civil War in Knaresborough and there are changing exhibitions in the Little Gallery.
   Open Etr, May–Sep, daily. Guided tours available.

▶ In AD 654 St Cedd built his monastery here in a place described by Bede as 'more like a place for lurking robbers and wild beasts than habitations for man'. The present Church of St Mary was built in 1078 on this site. There are three holy wells in the village, dedicated to St Chad, St Ovin and St Cedd.

LEEDS gazetteer

LEEDS
WEST YORKSHIRE. CITY OFF
M1, 170 MILES (274KM) NW
OF LONDON

▶ The city of Leeds is the largest urban development in Yorkshire and is certainly the economic capital of the county. It has become an important financial centre nationally and its constant growth is sustained by continuing relocation to Leeds of many national firms. In the 19th century Leeds owed its rapid development as an inland port to the Leeds–Liverpool and Aire and Calder canals, forming a link between Liverpool and Hull from where goods could be exported worldwide. Leeds became an important centre of the woollen industry and for ready-made clothing. The canal basin grew to provide extensive wharves, warehouses, boat-building yards and wet and dry docks until the railways and then roads took over as the main transport routes. However, like other cities with a similar Victorian heritage, interest has been rekindled in the long-neglected waterways and warehouses and Leeds Waterfront is now a stylish district with offices, shops, bars and restaurants. Granary Wharf has shops and a Sunday Festival Market in a canal side setting. A visitor centre is housed in the former canal office.

The main shopping areas of the city centre have been transformed by pedestrianisation, modernist landscaping and attractive lighting, and old Victorian shopping arcades and halls such as Kirkgate Market, the magnificently domed Corn Exchange and the Victorian Quarter have been restored to their former opulence. Kirkgate Market, a busy, traditional market, is particularly impressive with its extravagant domes and a mezzanine balcony supported by the 'Kirkgate Market Dragons'. The investment in the city centre has clearly paid off, since Leeds is now one of the most desirable retail locations in the country.

The Leeds Industrial Museum in Armley Mill, once the largest textile mill in the world, today houses a museum of the textile, clothing and engineering industries. The city's other industries also included clocks, chemicals and furniture-making. Thomas Chippendale began his furniture business here. Michael Marks, of Marks and Spencer, began his career at Leeds Penny Bazaar in Leeds Market, and in 1822 Joshua Tetley & Son was founded. The story of the brewery is told at Tetley's Brewery Wharf, a visitor attraction which also relates the history of the English pub.

The £42.5 million Royal Armouries Museum, in the Tower of Steel, is the first purpose-built national museum to be built in the 20th century, relocating most of the national collection of weapons and armour that has been stored at the Tower of London. Founded in 1988, Leeds City Art Gallery houses an excellent collection of works by Renoir, Lowry, Sickert and Leeds artist Atkinson Grimshaw.

Leeds has also developed as a major arts centre, home to Opera North, based at the city's Grand Theatre, the Northern School of

gazetteer

LEEDS

The magnificent Corn Exchange in Leeds

Contemporary Dance and the West Yorkshire Playhouse, which opened in 1990. The Henry Moore Institute, which opened in 1993, is the largest gallery in Europe devoted solely to sculpture.

Leeds has three important sporting venues: Elland Road, Leeds United Football Club; Headingly, Yorkshire County Cricket Club and, next door to it, Leeds Rugby League Club.

Armley Mills Industrial Museum
CANAL RD, ARMLEY. 2 MILES (3KM) W OF CITY CENTRE, OFF A65
TEL: 0113 263 7861

▶ Once the world's largest woollen mill, Armley Mills evokes memories of the 18th-century woollen industry, showing the progress of wool from the sheep to knitted clothing. The museum has its own 1920s cinema projection, including the first moving pictures taken in Leeds, as well as 1920s silent movies. Other attractions include demonstrations of static engines and steam locomotives, a printing gallery and a journey through the world of textiles and fashion.

Open all year, most days. Closed Mon (except BH).

City Art Gallery
THE HEADROW. CITY CENTRE, NEXT TO TOWN HALL AND LIBRARY
TEL: 0113 247 8248

▶ The City Art Gallery is home to one of the best collections of 20th-century British art outside London, as well as Victorian and late 19th-century pictures. It also has an outstanding collection of English watercolours, an exceptional display of modern sculpture and temporary exhibitions focusing on the modern and contemporary. Highlights include works by Holman Hunt, Andre Derain, Stanley Spencer, the Camden Town School, Henry Moore, Barbara Hepworth, Jacob Epstein, Cotman and Turner.

Open all year, daily. Closed BH.

LEEDS

gazetteer

▶ There is something for everyone in this museum, which has exhibits as diverse as a Bengal tiger, an Egyptian mummy, Roman remains, dinosaurs, fossils and minerals, and costumes and crafts from five continents. There is a programme of temporary exhibitions.

Open all year, most days.

▶ The most complete 12th-century Cistercian abbey in the country stands on the banks of the River Aire. The museum presents a colourful record of Victorian social life with reconstructed cobbled streets, shops and other attractions.

Open all year, most days. Abbey site open dawn–dusk.

▶ This was the first railway authorised by an Act of Parliament (in 1758) and the first to succeed with steam locomotives (in 1812). Steam trains run each weekend in season from Tunstall Road roundabout to Middleton Park. Facilities include a picnic area, nature trail and playgrounds. There is a programme of special events.

Moor Road Station open for viewing every wknd. Trains run wknds Apr–early Jan.

▶ Situated on the canal waterfront in the heart of Leeds, the museum is designed to bring to life the unique and magical history and development of arms and armour. The museum covers an area of 155,000 square feet (14,400sq m), displaying 20,000 items of the national collections. Touch-screen computers and live demonstrations add an extra dimension to the five galleries that tell the story of hunting, war, tournament, self-defence and the civilisations of Asia. A sixth, the news rooms, enables visitors to experience the excitement of a live television studio. Outside on the waterfront there is a 3,000 capacity tilt yard for jousting tournaments and Beating the Retreat. A craft court has demonstrations by skilled armourers and the training of hunting dogs and horses.

Open all year, daily. Closed Mon Nov–Feb.

▶ Described as 'the Hampton Court of the North' this Tudor and Jacobean mansion boasts extensive collections of decorative arts in their original room settings, including the incomparable Chippendale Collection. An extensive programme of renovation is restoring each room to its former glory, using original wall coverings and furniture. The house is set in 1,200 acres (485ha) of parkland landscaped by 'Capability' Brown. The gardens have magnificent seasonal displays; a riot of roses bloom in the vibrant borders in the old walled garden.

Open all year, most days. Limited winter opening.

City Museum
THE HEADROW
TEL: 0113 247 8275

Kirkstall Abbey and Abbey House Museum
ABBEY RD, KIRKSTALL. OFF A65, W OF CITY CENTRE
TEL: 0113 275 5821

Middleton Colliery Railway
MOOR RD, HUNSLET.
JUNC 45/M1 OR FOLLOW SIGNS FROM A61
TEL: 0113 271 0320
(ANSWERPHONE)

Royal Armouries Museum
ARMOURIES DR. OFF A61
CLOSE TO LEEDS CENTRE, FOLLOW BROWN TOURIST SIGNS
TEL: 0113 220 1999

Temple Newsam House & Park
OFF A63
TEL: 0113 264 7321
(HOUSE) & 264 5535 (PARK)

gazetteer

LEEDS–LEYBURN

Teltley's Brewery Wharf
THE WATERFRONT
TEL: 01132 242 0666

▶ Situated in the heart of Leeds, Tetley's Brewery Wharf introduces visitors to the fascinating history of the English pub. With the aid of elaborate sets and actors in period costume, visitors can experience life in a 14th-century ale house, through to Elizabethan, Jacobean, Georgian and Victorian hostelries, a 1940s blitzed pub and a futuristic pub. Crafts associated with the history of pubs are demonstrated – from inn sign painting to a cooper making traditional wooden barrels. Other attractions include an adventure playground, picnic area, restaurant, and an amphitheatre where a range of events is planned for the holiday season.

Open weekends only until end Mar. End Mar–Sep, daily.

Thwaite Mills
THWAITE LN, STOURTON.
2 MILES (3KM) S OF CITY
CENTRE, OFF A61
TEL: 0113 249 6453

▶ A knowledgeable guide takes visitors on a fascinating tour of this water-powered mill which sits between the River Aire and the Aire and Calder Navigation. Two great swishing wheels continually drive a mass of cogs and grinding wheels which crushed stone for putty and paint throughout the 19th century. This was the hub of a tiny island community; the Georgian mill-owner's house has been restored and today houses displays exploring the history of the mill. Visitors to Thwaite Mills can watch the story on video either before or after the guided tour. The tours start on the hour and last for approximately 45 minutes.

Open Mar–Dec, most days.

Tropical World
CANAL GARDENS, ROUNDHAY
PARK. 3 MILES (5KM) N OF CITY
CENTRE OFF A58 AT
OAKWOOD
TEL: 0113 266 1850

▶ Adjacent to Canal Gardens is Tropical World, one of the UK's most visited garden attractions. The atmosphere of the tropics is re-created as visitors walk among banana, citrus, pineapple and other exotic trees. A waterfall cascades into a rock pool at the rate of 1,000 gallons (4,546 litres) a minute and other pools are home to terrapins and carp. Elsewhere are many displays of live reptiles and exotic insects. In the Butterfly House more than 30 species can be seen feeding off the plants. There is also a Nocturnal House, a South American Rainforest (containing a wide range of exotic orchids) and a Desert House with specimens of cacti and succulents gathered from the deserts of the world.

Open all year, daily.

LEYBURN
NORTH YORKSHIRE. SMALL
TOWN ON A6108, 8 MILES
(13KM) SW OF RICHMOND

▶ Leyburn, the administrative centre for the area, is a busy but spacious town with a flourishing market, craft shops, and a modern auction house which holds general and specialist sales. The most notable buildings are the Bolton Arms and Leyburn Hall. A walk from Shawl Terrace, at the top of the Market Place, leads to Leyburn Shawl, a limestone terrace which has glorious views of Wensleydale.

▶ Tall trees, a babbling beck and grassy banks are the setting for the exceptionally grand – for such a modest village – Fountaine Hospital, almshouses founded in 1721. Richard Fountaine, it is said, was in the timber trade, went to London and made his fortune during the Black Death. The almshouses are classical, very much in the style of Vanbrugh's Castle Howard (see page 46), which was being constructed at the time not far away. It has been suggested that Fountaine's builder was someone who was also involved in Castle Howard, possibly William Etty (1675–1734). The façade is in fact deceptive, for the building behind is not extensive. Fountaine's name is also commemorated in the tiny pub, standing among trees on the village's irregularly shaped, sloping green. At the foot of the green a ford, stepping stones and three bridges cross the little river, one an ancient clapper bridge, another a 14th-century packhorse bridge and the third a modern road bridge. All around the green are soft limestone houses. Linton Hall is an excellent house that dates basically from the 17th century but has later additions. It has a pretty Dutch-gabled doorway. The church is mainly Norman and delightful, a little way away from the centre of its captivating village.

▶ Litton is a very picturesque village grouped around a green and with a stream running through it. There is a footbridge over the River Skirfare and footpaths along the river banks. Littondale is a valley of great beauty and is largely unspoilt, one of the few valleys unscarred by lead-mining. The valley has also been used as the setting for the television series *Emmerdale*.

▶ Built in Edwardian times, the former home of the Gascoigne family is now a country house museum. It contains furniture, pictures, silver and ceramics from the Gascoigne collection, and works of art on loan from Leeds galleries. Other attractions include a gallery of Oriental art, a display of British fashion, contemporary crafts and frequent special exhibitions. Outside, the Edwardian garden, bird garden and deer park are delightful places in which to stroll.
Open Mar–Dec, most days.

▶ The village, although popular with tourists, manages to retain its ancient, picturesque charm, with many of the farmhouses and cottages dating from the 17th century. Just outside the village is the spectacular 'Great Scar' limestone scenery with the famous natural features of Malham Cove, the great cliff of Gordale Scar, the dry bed of a waterfall and Malham Tarn. The remains of an Iron Age settlement can be seen close by.

LINTON IN CRAVEN
NORTH YORKSHIRE. VILLAGE ON B6265, 1 MILE (2KM) S OF GRASSINGTON

LITTON
NORTH YORKSHIRE. VILLAGE OFF B6160, 2 MILES (3KM) NW OF ARNCLIFFE

LOTHERTON HALL
WEST YORKSHIRE. OFF THE A1, ¾ MILE (1KM) E OF JUNC WITH B1217
TEL: 0113 281 3259

MALHAM
NORTH YORKSHIRE. VILLAGE OFF A65, 5 MILES (8KM) E OF SETTLE

gazetteer

MALHAM–MALTON

Yorkshire Dales National Park Centre
TEL: *01729 830363*

▶ The national park centre has maps, guides and local information, together with displays on the remarkable natural history of the area, local community and work of conservation bodies. Audio-visual presentations are provided for groups and a 24-hour teletext information service is available.

Open Apr–Oct, daily. Limited winter opening.

MALTON
NORTH YORKSHIRE. TOWN OFF A64, 17 MILES (27KM) NE OF YORK

▶ Malton has been the historic centre of Ryedale since Roman times. North of the Roman fort site is the original town of Old Malton, with ancient stone houses and quaint dwellings, in the centre of which stands St Mary's, the only remaining Gilbertine priory in England. Alongside farming, brewing is a traditional Malton industry.

Castle Howard
15 MILES (24KM) NW OF YORK, OFF A64
TEL: *01653 648333*

▶ In its dramatic setting of lakes, fountains and extensive gardens, this 18th-century palace was designed by Sir John Vanbrugh. Principal location for the television series *Brideshead Revisited*, this was the first major achievement of the architect who later created the lavish Blenheim Palace near Oxford. Castle Howard was begun in 1699 for the 3rd Earl of Carlisle, Charles Howard, whose descendants still call the place 'home'. The striking façade is topped by an 80-foot (24m) painted and gilded dome. The interior has a 192-foot (28m) Long Gallery, as well as a chapel with magnificent stained-glass windows by the 19th-century artist, Edward Burne-Jones. Besides the collections of antique furniture, porcelain and sculpture, the castle contains a number of important paintings, including a portrait of Henry VIII by Holbein and works by Rubens, Reynolds and Gainsborough. The grounds include the domed Temple of the Four Winds by Vanbrugh, and the richly designed family Mausoleum by Hawksmoor. The Rose Garden contains both old-fashioned and modern varieties of roses. Ray Wood is a 30-acre (12ha) area with unique collections of rare trees, and shrubs including rhododendrons and azaleas.

Open 1st 2 weeks of Mar, grounds only; mid Mar–Oct, grounds, plant centre and house open.

(See also Walk: Three Pyramids at Castle Howard, opposite.)

Eden Camp Modern History Theme Museum
EDEN CAMP, JUNC OF A64 & A169
TEL: *01653 697777*

▶ The story of the people's war – the drama, the hardships, the humour – unfolds in this museum devoted to civilian life in World War II. The displays, covering the blackout, rationing, the Blitz, the Homeguard and others, are housed in a former prisoner-of-war camp built in 1942 for German and Italian soldiers. Hut 29 depicts the military and political events of 1944, with a special section covering D-Day. Hut 11 is a children's 'hands-on' educational theme centre.

Open mid Jan–Dec, most days.

THREE PYRAMIDS AT CASTLE HOWARD

Walk

From the village of Welburn this walk visits some of the more unusual buildings on the Castle Howard Estate.

Grid ref: SE727677

INFORMATION
The walk is about 4½ miles (7km) long.
Some sections may be muddy.
Several stiles.
Pub in Welburn; café and other facilities for visitors at Castle Howard.

START
Welburn is off the A64, south-west of Malton. Park carefully at the roadside by Chestnut Avenue in Welburn.

DIRECTIONS
Take the bridleway, where the houses begin, and continue for 440yds (402m) to a field entrance. Turn left along a track, with a hedge on the right, and descend to a gate. Pass through, and follow the path through woodland. At a fork, bear right to cross a stile, then go uphill to the Four Faces. Continue straight ahead for 400yds (365m) to see the Pyramid in Pretty Wood. Return to the Four Faces and turn right, to follow the track for ½ mile (1km). Where it bends right to a gate, you can see beyond to the

Castle Howard is one of Britain's finest stately homes

Walk

THREE PYRAMIDS AT CASTLE HOWARD

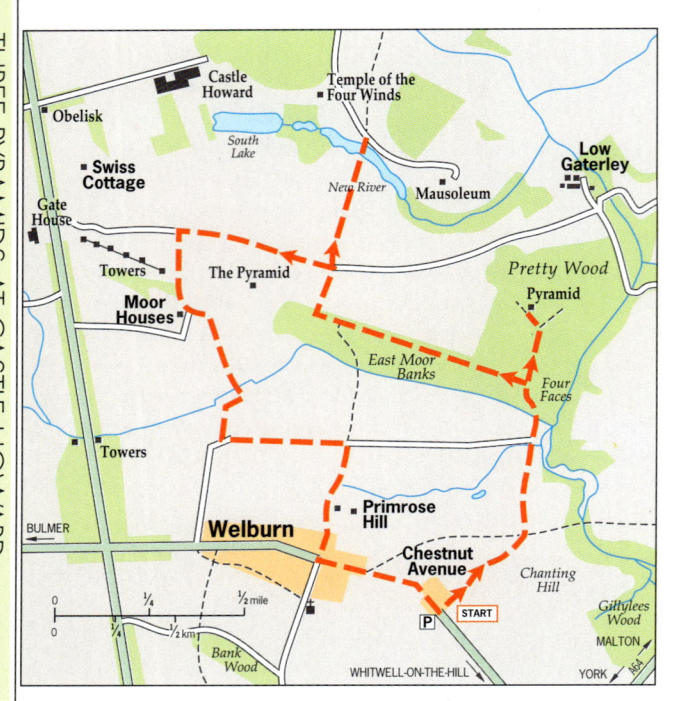

Great Pyramid, the dome of Castle Howard, and the Mausoleum. Descend to a road; turn left and immediately right down a track to the bridge, for great views of Castle Howard and the bridge. Return to the road and turn right, passing the Pyramid. Another pyramid is seen ahead, above a gateway. Take a signed track to the left, past a ruined tower, and follow another sign diagonally left downhill across the field (no obvious path) to the end of a small wood, and cross a stile in the trees. Head towards a corrugated iron barn – this section of the route may be muddy. Follow the hedge round to the left by farm buildings and cross a stile. Turn right (arrowed), with a hedge to your right, towards Welburn church spire. Go over two more stiles to reach and cross a third, which is set in a wire mesh fence. Bear right around the field edge until the fence turns right, then follow right around the edge of the field to a track. Turn left along the track, and continue for 440yds (402m) to a junction of tracks by an oak tree. Turn right here towards Welburn, and continue to meet a lane. Go straight on, and at the main road turn left, to return to the start point.

Castle Howard

The great 18th-century palace of Castle Howard was designed by Sir John Vanbrugh, and is familiar from its starring television roles in *Brideshead Revisited* and *The Buccaneers*. The dome was the first to be built on a private house in England. The grounds are also magnificent, with a number of family memorials, including the Great Pyramid. The Pyramid Gate was built in 1719, and both the Pyramid in Pretty Wood and the Four Faces some time before 1727.

The Temple of the Four Winds, near the bridge, is on the former main street of the village of Henderskelfe, which was demolished when the castle was built. The Ruined Tower, a folly, is part of Vanbrugh's medieval-style estate wall. The Mausoleum is a masterpiece by Vanbrugh's young assistant, Nicholas Hawksmoor. (See also page 46.)

WHAT TO LOOK OUT FOR

Castle Howard's landscape is designed to resemble an Italian painting. Notice the Great Pyramid's eight stone lanterns, the Temple's fine urns, and the openings in the bridge's balustrade that match the shape of the mausoleum, with its 20 columns.

MASHAM–MIDDLEHAM

gazetteer

▶ This market town, on the River Ure, was granted its market charter by Richard II in 1393. The annual sheep fair was revived a few years ago. The town is home to Theakston's Brewery, famed for its Old Peculier brew. There is a visitors' centre at the brewery.

▶ At the visitor centre adjacent to the Brewery visitors can discover how Theakston's Traditional ales are brewed and see the ancient skills of the cooper, together with an exclusive video, a museum and a gift shop.
Open Mar–Oct, most days.

▶ The monks of Jervaulx founded Middleham's main industry when they began training their horses on the Low Moor just above the village. By the late-18th century there were race meetings held on the moor and the first racing stables had been established. The village has two market crosses, one in each square.

▶ Middleham is dominated by the 12th-century keep (English Heritage) which saw its great days during the Wars of the Roses. The seat of the Neville family, the Earls of Warwick, it was the home for a time of the young King Richard III, then Duke of Gloucester, who married the Earl's daughter Anne Neville.
Open all year, Apr–Oct, daily, Nov–Mar certain days. Closed 24–26 Dec & 1 Jan.

MASHAM
NORTH YORKSHIRE. SMALL TOWN ON A6108, 8 MILES (13KM) NW OF RIPON

Theakston Brewery Visitor Centre
THE BREWERY. ON A6108
TEL: 01765 689057

MIDDLEHAM
NORTH YORKSHIRE. VILLAGE ON A6108, 2 MILES (3KM) SE OF LEYBURN

Middleham Castle
TEL: 01969 623899

The remains of the Norman castle at Middleham

gazetteer

MIDDLESTOWN–MUKER

MIDDLESTOWN NATIONAL COAL MINING MUSEUM FOR ENGLAND
WEST YORKSHIRE. CAPHOUSE COLLIERY, NEW RD. ON A642 BETWEEN WAKEFIELD AND HUDDERSFIELD
TEL: 01924 848806

▶ A unique opportunity to go 450 feet (137m) underground down one of Britain's oldest working mine shafts, where models and machinery depict methods and conditions of mining from the early 1800s to the present day. Visitors are strongly advised to wear sensible footwear and warm clothing. Other attractions include surface displays (both indoor and outdoor), pit ponies, 'paddy' train rides, a steam winder, a nature trail and an adventure playground. Special events take place throughout the year.

Open all year, daily. Closed 24–26 Dec & 1 Jan.

MORLEY
WEST YORKSHIRE. TOWN OFF M62, 4 MILES (6KM) SW OF LEEDS

▶ The earliest mention of Morley is in the Domesday Book, as Moreleia, meaning 'fields of the moor'. The town was built around seven hills and grew with the cotton industry. Prime Minister Asquith was born here.

MUKER
NORTH YORKSHIRE. VILLAGE ON B6270, 8 MILES (13KM) W OF REETH

▶ The village lies at the foot of Kisdon Hill in Upper Swaledale. The Church of St Mary is the focal point of the village and the grey stone houses huddle around it in a group. Today, the village enjoys prosperity from wool, and in particular Swaledale Woollens, where garments are handknitted by the villagers from wool of the local Swaledale sheep.

A flower meadow at Muker

NEWBY HALL & GARDENS

gazetteer

A quiet corner in the gardens at Newby Hall

In the 17th century the gardener was the most highly paid of the Newby Hall staff, earning £16 a year. The cook was second at £10 and the brewer earned £8, twice as much as the butler, who was then some way down the hierarchy of domestic staff. The poor poultry maid had to manage on £1.15s.

▶ The early history of Newby Hall is something of a mystery, although a property was recorded here in the 13th century. The present house dates from the late-17th century and was built for William Weddell, who had returned from his Grand Tour of Europe with such a large collection of works of art that he needed a suitably grand home in which to display them to proper effect. Among his purchases were superb classical sculptures and a set of Gobelin tapestries.

When it came to designing a suitable setting for Weddell's treasures, one name sprang immediately to mind and that was Robert Adam, the foremost classical architect of his age. The entrance hall, library and sculpture gallery show his work at its very best, and the wonderful Tapestry Room, surviving in its entirety, demonstrates Adam's skill at creating unity between the décor and contents of the room.

Other rooms have developed over the years to suit the needs of the succession of owners and are a delightful mixture of styles and colour schemes, but the recently decorated drawing room has gone back to Adam's original scheme. The dining room is an elegant Regency addition to Newby Hall, and the lovely gardens which surround the house were largely created by the present owner's father.

Open Apr–Sep, most afternoons.

NEWBY HALL & GARDENS
NORTH YORKSHIRE. 4 MILES (6.5KM) SE OF RIPON & 2 MILES (3KM) W OF A1. OFF B6265, BETWEEN BOROUGHBRIDGE AND RIPON TEL: 01423 322583

51

gazetteer

THE NORTH YORK MOORS

The North York Moors covers an area of predominantly limestone and sandstone scenery which contains the largest unbroken stretch of heather moorland in England. In late summer the heather covers the park's rolling landscape in a carpet of purple, but the moors themselves, divided by wooded river valleys, are far from uniform. In Levisham Moor to the south is the Hole of Horcum, a vast natural amphitheatre formed by the action of underground springs, and east of Grime Moor along Dovedale Griff are windcarved sandstone outcrops, just one of a number of rock formations on the moors that are known as the Bridestones.

Down the park's eastern border lies a stretch of Heritage Coast, along which huddle the picturesque villages of Runswick Bay, Robin Hood's Bay and Staithes, where Captain James Cook was once an apprentice. The Cleveland coast is one of the fastest eroding coasts in England and its dramatic heights include Boulby Cliff, the highest point on the east coast of England at 666 feet (202m). Just inland from the towering cliffs, and in stark contrast to them, is Boulby Potash Mine which boasts the deepest mine shaft in England.

Along the park's southern boundary are the Tabular Hills, which rise from the Vale of Pickering and gain their name from the flat, table-like nature of their summits. On the park's western border are the steep Hambleton Hills containing one of the few surviving moorland lakes, Lake Gormire, enclosed within a landslip. South of here, carved into Roulston Scar is the striking landmark of the White Horse of Kilburn marked out by white-stone chippings. Despite the hills within its boundary the park is a relatively low-lying area, its highest point standing at 1,490 feet (454m) in the west, near the long-distance walk of the Cleveland Way.

THE NORTH YORK MOORS — gazetteer

The scenery of the moors is littered with the remains of man's involvement with the area. Stretching across Wheeldale Moor is a belt of heather-covered stones, the foundations of the Roman Wade's Causeway, and throughout the region numerous moorland crosses mark ancient forest boundaries and memorial sites. Of these, the elegant Ralph Cross, high on Westerdale Moor, has been used as the national park's symbol. Monasteries and castles within the park date from the Norman period. Chief amongst these are the stone skeleton of Rievaulx Abbey, and to the south-west the snag-toothed remains of Byland Abbey. The ruins of Helmsley Castle, besieged by the Parliamentarians during the Civil War, can still be seen at Helmsley.

Two railway lines run through the park. The Esk Valley line runs from Battersby to Whitby, and the privately owned North Yorkshire Moors Railway line through Newtondale, carrying steam engines along one

Ralph Cross was chosen as the emblem of the North York Moors National Park

gazetteer

THE NORTH YORK MOORS

The distinctive profile of Roseberry Topping is a landmark for miles around

of the oldest lines in the world. Along with Boulby Mine, the stone arches of ironstone mines on Rosedale Moor testify to the park's industrial heritage. In the north-west Roseberry Topping's distinctive lopsided peak is partly due to the collapse of mines below it, after it was exploited for its alum, iron-ore, jet and roadstone.

There are a number of nature reserves within the park including the steep, wooded Forge Valley through which the River Derwent flows. During April thousands of daffodils cover the banks of the River Dove in Farndale, an area designated a Local Nature Reserve. The open moors, the eastern cliffs, the coniferous plantations, and the enclosed farming country are the natural habitats for a variety of animal species. The rare merlin makes its home here and the red grouse (confined to England) is reared upon the moors. Recently however, the planting of large areas of conifers and the reclamation of moors for improved agriculture has meant a steady reduction in the park's moorland.

NORTON CONYERS—NOSTELL PRIORY

gazetteer

▶ The history of the Grahams of Norton Conyers is one of ups and downs. A wild and unruly bunch, they came from Scotland in the early-17th century. However, one younger son went to London in the service of the Duke of Buckingham, rose to be one of Charles I's Gentlemen of the Horse and came back a baronet. Loyalty to the Crown cost them dearly after the Civil War, but the Restoration brought new honour and several royal visits to their home. The 4th Baronet was poisoned, albeit accidentally, and the 7th squandered away the family fortune and most of its property, including Norton Conyers. Fortunately his son married an heiress and was able to buy it back.

The house has seen many changes since it was first built in the mid-14th century, with substantial alterations being carried out towards the end of the 18th century. There are fine portraits all around the house and some excellent pieces of furniture, including the long table in the hall which dates from the Middle Ages. The library contains a collection of costumes dating from the 1880s, and further costumes and family wedding dresses are on show in the 'best' spare room. King James's Room, where James II stayed when he was Duke of York, is furnished in 17th-century style.

Open Jun–mid Sep, selected days.

▶ Built by Paine in the middle of the 18th century, the priory (National Trust) has an additional wing built by Adam in 1766. It contains a notable saloon and tapestry room and displays pictures and Chippendale furniture. There is a lake in the grounds. Events, including a country fair, are held in the grounds.

Open end Apr–Oct, certain days.

NORTON CONYERS
NORTH YORKSHIRE. 3½ MILES (5.5KM) NW OF RIPON
TEL: 01765 640333

Sheep graze the lawns at Nostell Priory, below

NOSTELL PRIORY
WEST YORKSHIRE 6 MILES (9.5KM) SE OF WAKEFIELD, OFF A638
TEL: 01924 863892

Walk

OAKWELL HALL

Though close to the roaring traffic of the M62, this walk enters a different world – of an Elizabethan stone and timber country house with a lovely walled garden, amidst the open spaces and pleasant footpaths of a modern country park.

Grid ref: SE212269

INFORMATION
The walk is just under 2 miles (3km) long.
Mainly easy walking.
Information centre at car park.
Café and exhibition areas in converted farm buildings by hall.
Picnic area with play area between the car park and the hall.
Toilets at the car park (with baby changing room) and at the hall.

START
There is a large, free car park on the A652 between Bradford and Dewsbury, reached from the M62 (junction 26) via the A58.

DIRECTIONS
From the country park entrance and car park, take the wide track ahead beyond the information centre, by the wooden gate. This path crosses a broad field (part of a reclaimed colliery) and leads steeply down to a bridge over Oakwell Beck. Cross, and walk up the steps towards the garden in front of Oakwell Hall with its little statue of a ram.

15th-century Oakwell Hall

OAKWELL HALL

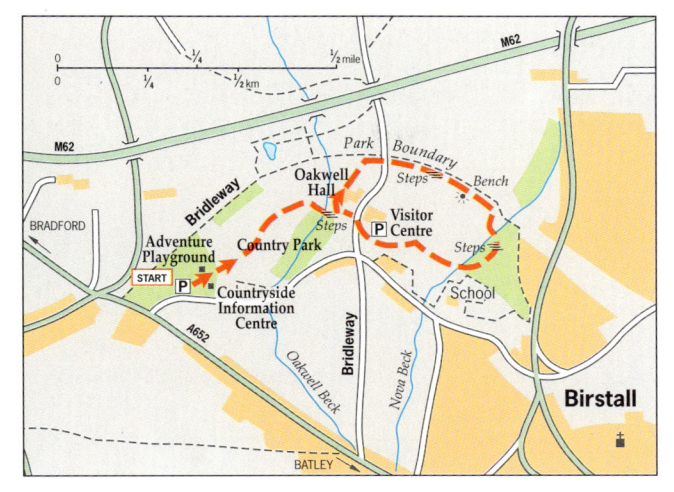

Walk

the path in front of the hall, taking the steps down to Oakwell Beck and retrace your steps to the start.

Oakwell Hall

The hall, faithfully refurnished in period style, was a mid 15th-century timber yeoman's house which was later encased in stone by a prosperous local landowner, John Batt. Look for the date over the door. The house has remained largely unchanged for 350 years.

Open all year, daily.
Tel: 01924 326240.

Unless you are going into the hall, take the path to the left of the house, alongside the walled garden behind the hall and past the wildlife garden. Continue past the arboretum to reach the old railway, and go up a fenced path back to the old railway bridge. Turn right along the footpath alongside the old railway cutting (avoid the horse track). After 50 yards (46m) climb steps, at the top of which is a seat with a fine view across Oakwell Hall and Country Park and the Spen Valley, with the tall television mast on Emley Moor a notable landmark.

The path soon descends past birch trees. At a crossroads take the narrow path descending to the right, parallel with the stream, past oak and birch woods, soon crossing a wooden footbridge to the woods.

Keep on the main path, but soon take a crossing path to the right, which leads to another footbridge over the stream, then cross the bridleway (watch out for galloping horses). Cross the field ahead on the pathway, but keep inside the next field wall before bearing left into a picnic area, and up a stone ramp into the car park.

Keep straight ahead towards Oakwell Hall and Visitor Centre. Return along

The chiffchaff, a common bird of trees and scrub

WHAT TO LOOK OUT FOR

The Tudor/Jacobean style herb garden by the hall entrance contains a variety of culinary and medicinal herbs, while the old walled garden has been laid out in formal style, with old roses and other plants and shrubs of the period. There are lots of interesting things to see in the woods, scrub and grassland of the country park. Woodland birds are common among the oaks and silver birches, and waterside plants flourish along the streams. A nature trail leaflet is available.

gazetteer

OSMOTHERLEY – PARCEVALL HALL GARDENS

OSMOTHERLEY
NORTH YORKSHIRE. VILLAGE OFF A19, 6 MILES (10KM) NW OF NORTHALLERTON

Mount Grace Priory
1 MILE (1.5KM) NW OF OSMOTHERLEY
TEL: 01609 883494

OTLEY
WEST YORKSHIRE. TOWN ON A660, 10 MILES (16KM) NW OF LEEDS

PARCEVALL HALL GARDENS
NORTH YORKSHIRE. OFF B6265 BETWEEN GRASSINGTON AND PATELEY BRIDGE
TEL: 01756 720311

RIVER OUSE
Unusually, there is only one accepted source of the River Ouse, marked by an obelisk in the grounds of a seed warehouse at Great Ouseburn. The river is tidal to Naburn Lock, and commercial traffic still reaches York. Although remote from the main cruising network, the reaches above York are much used by local pleasure craft.

▶ This beautifully preserved village in the North York Moors National Park makes a good centre for exploring the surrounding heather moorland. The village is dominated by the Mount Grace Priory (English Heritage), founded in 1398, and Britain's finest example of a Carthusian monastery.

▶ The ruined 14th-century Carthusian priory (English Heritage) stands next to a 17th-century house. One of the monks' cells has been fully restored to show where the monks lived and worked in solitude, and what life was like in this monastery. There are also extensive remains of the cloister, church and outer court.
   Open all year, Apr–Oct, daily; Nov–Mar, certain days. Closed 24–26 Dec & 1 Jan.

▶ The parish church, dedicated to All Saints, has a fine Norman doorway and fragments of Anglo-Saxon crosses. The market, held on Fridays and Saturdays, dates from Saxon times although the charter was granted in 1222. The Wharfedale Agricultural Show has been held at Otley since 1799. Thomas Chippendale, the cabinet maker, was born here in 1718.

▶ Enjoying a hillside setting east of the main Wharfedale Valley, these beautiful gardens belong to an Elizabethan house which is used as the Bradford Diocesan Retreat House (not open to the public).
   Open Good Fri–Oct, daily. Winter by appointment.

PATELEY BRIDGE—THE PENNINES

gazetteer

▶ Pateley Bridge is a thriving Dales town on the banks of the River Nidd with a steep High Street. The town gets its name from the river crossing first used by the monks of Fountains Abbey; the present stone bridge dates from the 18th century. The Upper Nidderdale Museum, situated in an original Victorian workhouse, portrays the life of the early Dalesfolk. To the west of Pateley Bridge, on the B6265, are the Stump Cross Caverns where an impressive show cave has beautiful displays of colour-illuminated stalactites, stalagmites and crystal formations.

▶ Known as 'the backbone of England', the Pennines run the length of northern England, dividing Yorkshire and Cumbria. The range of hills is 145 miles (233km) in length and varies between 20 miles (32km) and 40 miles (64km) in width, forming the main watershed of northern England. Little of the range rises above 2,000 feet (610m) and most of it is between 100 feet (30.5m) and 1,500 feet (457m) in height.

The Southern Pennines end in the Edale Valley with a limestone plateau with ridges of acid moorland down each side often edged with long thin crags of millstone grit. The Central Pennines, from the Edale Valley to the Aire Gap, are a region of high millstone grit hills which create a bleak and boggy landscape of endless moorland. The Northern Pennines continue for another 70 miles (112km) to the Tyne Valley and the landscape becomes more dramatic, with cliffs such as Malham Cove and Kilnsey Crag, limestone pavements and the highest point of the Pennines in the Cross Fell and Mickle Fell massif.

The Pennine Way is one of Britain's most famous long-distance walks.

PATELEY BRIDGE
NORTH YORKSHIRE. SMALL TOWN ON B6165, 11 MILES (18KM) NW OF HARROGATE

THE PENNINES
WEST YORKSHIRE. HILL RANGE

Opposite, Mount Grace Priory is the best preserved of the nine Carthusian monasteries that were built in England

Below, dry-stone walls are a feature of the Pennines

gazetteer

PICKERING

PICKERING
NORTH YORKSHIRE. TOWN ON A170, 16 MILES (26KM) W OF SCARBOROUGH

North Yorkshire Moors Railway
PICKERING STATION
TEL: 01751 472508

▶ Pickering is the largest of Rydale's market towns, set on the narrow, fertile plain of the Vale of Pickering. Once an important coaching stop, there are numerous medieval inns and an old cattle market which now houses the tourist information centre. Standing upon its mound high above the town, the 12th-century keep and baileys of Pickering Castle (English Heritage) are all that is left of this favourite royal hunting lodge. There is an exhibition on the castle's history.

▶ The scenery enjoyed by visitors to the North Yorkshire Moors Railway is some of the finest on any preserved railway. The 18-mile (29km) railway can be reached by the charming branch line that runs from the shadows of the transporter bridge at Middlesbrough through Eskdale to Whitby. The interchange at Grosmont is almost across the platform.

If you are not arriving by rail, there is more parking space available at Pickering, and the nearby Beck Isle Museum provides an introduction to life on the North York Moors. The attractive stone station building is the first of many fine period structures on the line, including goods sheds and signal boxes.

For the first half of the one-hour journey, the railway closely follows the course of Pickering Beck through roadless Newton Dale. This unspoilt valley was scoured out by glacial action and offers walkers many opportunities, which are indicated on information boards at Levisham and Newtondale stations. Soon after the train leaves the passing loop at Levisham, the architectural folly of Skelton Tower can be seen to the right, erected by an eccentric Victorian vicar of the same name. The steep climb up the valley continues to Newtondale, where passengers need to request a stop. A waymarked path leads through the woods to the west of the line back to Levisham where walkers can continue their rail journey. Beyond Newtondale the gradient eases as the train leaves the forest behind and enters a section of open moorland.

At Eller Beck the line is crossed by the Lyke Wake Walk, which links the coast at Ravenscar with Osmotherley. The observant eye will detect traces of an abandoned railway formation on the west side of the line, which was the course of the railway until 1865 when the present line was built to eliminate a major hindrance to the railway – the inclined plane from Goathland to Beck Hole near Grosmont. Horses, then locomotives, hauled carriages and waggons to the foot of the incline, which was operated by cable powered by a stationary steam engine.

It is well worth breaking the journey at Goathland – the station is the most attractive on the line, with some fine North Eastern Railway signals, a Historic Railway Trail leading to the route of the incline, with boards explaining its history and the significance of the remains, and

PICKERING gazetteer

Passengers enjoying the glorious scenery of the North Yorkshire Moors Railway

for the energetic there are some of the best walks the North York Moors has to offer. A circular walk, for which boots are needed, takes you past the celebrated Mallyan Spout waterfall and one of the best-preserved stretches of Roman road on Wheeldale Moor.

The descent of the line to Grosmont is one of the loveliest sections, dropping down through the woods and criss-crossing Eller Beck before it joins the Murk Esk at Beck Hole. The noise and steam of ascending trains as they struggle up the fearsome 1-in-49 gradient is one of the most stirring sounds and sights to be enjoyed on a preserved railway. This is the place for some excellent photo-opportunities, with plenty of good angles for photographers.

As you near Goathland, the long line of the Esk Valley cottages and the trackbed of the old line can be seen to the left. Soon after, the railway's locomotive workshops and depot can be seen on the right. A whistle from the locomotive and you plunge into the double-track tunnel that brings the train to journey's end.

The history of this railway is particularly interesting. The Whitby & Pickering was an early line, built by the 'father of British railways', George Stephenson, and opened with the noisy celebration of five bands and 7,000 people in 1836. A book in tribute to the railway was published in the same year – *The Scenery of the Whitby & Pickering Railway* – illustrated by G H Dodgson who was apprenticed to Stephenson.

Events throughout the year include Friends of Thomas the Tank Engine and a Steam Gala.

Train service: Apr–Oct, daily; Santa Specials in Dec, service between Xmas and New Year.

Cycle ride

LANES AND VILLAGES OF THE EAST YORKSHIRE WOLDS

This is likely to be a whole day's ride, on lanes lightly-trafficked even on summer Sundays, providing a tranquil countryside experience. Views from the high points take in the broad Vale of York as far as the Humber and Trent. Most of the climbs are easily graded, the few steeper ones being quite short, though care is needed on some of the sinuous narrow descents. Opportunities arise along the way to shorten the excursion if necessary.

INFORMATION

Total Distance
23½ miles (38km)

Grade
Challenging

OS Map
Landranger 1:50,000 sheet 106 (Market Weighton)

Tourist Information
No TIC at or near start. Local information: Town Clerk, tel: 01759 304851; Beverley/York

Cycle Shops/Hire
Wheelies, Pocklington, tel: 01759 304353

Nearest Railway Station
York (13 miles/21km)

Refreshments
Pocklington has cafés, tea rooms, pubs and a noted Austrian restaurant. Food is also available at the shop/tea garden at Londesborough and the Ramblers' Rest, Millington. There are pubs in only two villages: Bishop Wilton and Millington; both serve food. Just off the route is Millington Wood picnic area and nature reserve.

START

Pocklington is a market town just north of the A1079 York to Hull road, 13 miles (21km) east of York. Parking is free behind the old railway station (Sports Hall) on Station Road off the roundabout near Safeway. Start the ride from a layby leading off the roundabout to Burnby Hall Park and Gardens.

DIRECTIONS

1. From the layby in Pocklington, go west on the Balk for 110 yards (100m), turn right into New Street taking the first right into Burnby Lane, signposted 'Burnby 3'. Continue on this narrow lane for about 3 miles (5km) to Burnby. In the village turn sharp right by the church, signed 'Londesborough', and continue over a beck out of the village, climbing gently for about 1 mile (1.5km) to a T-junction where you turn right. After a further mile (1.5km) go straight over a crossroads into the village of Londesborough, descend and bear left to the church; continue to the end of the street, take a sharp turn left, climb for 110 yards (100m) then take the first left to the shop/tea room. Turn right here to the crossroads to go north following the signs for 'Warter'.

2. After leaving Londesborough, climb gently to a crossroads and turn right, signposted 'Middleton'. To shorten the route, keep ahead at the crossroads to Nunburnholme, then bear left into the village. Otherwise continue for 2 miles (3km), turn left at the T-junction signposted 'Warter' and descend with care to Warter. Once there, turn left at the junction with the B1246 into the

LANES AND VILLAGES OF THE EAST YORKSHIRE WOLDS

Cycle ride

All Saints' Church, Londesborough

village and fork left before the memorial. Shortly bear left on Mill Lane, signed 'Nunburnholme', descend to cross a beck and go up a short ascent. Continue on a narrow lane for 1¼ miles (2km) before turning right at a T-junction (give way). Descend to Nunburnholme, bearing left into the village, with the church at the far south-west end.

3. Fork right at a bus shelter, signed 'Pocklington', and continue to a junction with the B1246. Turn left towards Pocklington then right (take great care here), rising to Kilnwick Percy. In 1 mile (1.5km), at spot height 108m, bear left following a narrow lane down to Beck Cottage. Climb to Millington, going right at a T-junction. Take the first left opposite with care, pass the church and turn right to a crossroads. Turn left (not signposted), then take the first left opposite a café, passing a church, where you go right to a crossroads. Turn left here (no signpost), at the Balk, climbing to soon reach a T-junction. Note: if conditions are very wet or time is short, turn left to Pocklington.

4. Continue ahead along a farm track/bridleway, passing Little Givendale Farm. Follow bridleway signs (blue arrow on yellow) through two gates, then proceed north-west through pasture to a steep descent (or walk) into Whitekeld Dale. Cross a gated bridge and continue on the bridleway for ½ mile (1km) to the church at Great Givendale.

On reaching a road beyond, cross over into Givendale village, continuing past a manor house. With care, descend this narrow winding lane for ½ mile (1km) to a T-junction.

5. To visit Bishop Wilton 2 miles (3km) on, turn right at this junction and retrace. Otherwise, turn left, signed 'Pocklington', continue for 1 mile (1.5km) to Meltonby, and go straight ahead, signposted 'Yapham'. After a further 1 mile (1.5km), at the next junction, go through Yapham, and forward to the next crossroads at Yapham Grange. Turn left and on to Pocklington, entering by Sherbuttgate. Near the church, fork right to a mini-roundabout and forward on Station Road to a large roundabout and the car park.

PLACES OF INTEREST

Pocklington
This small market town with a leisurely air has broad squares and wide streets; market day is Tuesday and early closing Wednesday. Its 13th-century church with 15th-century Perpendicular tower is visible from miles around. Slave reformer William Wilberforce was a pupil at the public school here. Burnby Hall Gardens is the town's most noted amenity. It features the Stewart Collection, a remarkable

LANES AND VILLAGES OF THE EAST YORKSHIRE WOLDS

Cycle ride

LANES AND VILLAGES OF THE EAST YORKSHIRE WOLDS

A leafy lane near Pocklington

display of trophies and artefacts collected by Major Stewart during seven world tours from 1906 to 1926. The lake has one of the finest collections of water lilies in Europe, and there is a seat dedicated to G H Stancer, OBE, born here in 1878 and for 25 years Secretary of the Cyclists' Touring Club.

Burnby

Well worth seeing is the small Church of St Giles, with its fine Norman-style doorway and west end and bellcote rebuilt in 1840. Beyond the village Burnby chalk pit can be discerned from far across the vale, though the distinctive Cleaving Combe is easily missed.

Londesborough

An estate village associated with the Burlington's fine park, this was said to be the location of the Northumbrian kings' summer palace, and where Edwin met Paulinus in AD 627. After passing to the Cavendishes and later the 6th Duke of Devonshire, the hall was pulled down in 1819. The park is laid out with superb lakes, waterfalls and terraces, along with extensive avenues. It was sold in 1845 to the notorious 'Railway King', George Hudson, who was then planning the railway from York to Market Weighton, and included his private station on the park's edge. The hall's foundations and terraces can still be seen from the park gates, and there are public footpaths and bridleways through the private estate. All Saints' Church is largely Early English, but has a Norman south doorway with an Anglo-Danish 11th-century crosshead. Its white limestone porch has a sundial of 1764.

Kilnwick Percy

When seen from the B1246, Kilnwick Percy Hall is impressive, with its estate lake and the tiny St Helen's Church. The hall, which today is a Buddhist Centre, was once part of the extensive estate held by the Percy family in Yorkshire. To the north, Home Farm is an intriguing collection of buildings.

Bishop Wilton

Sheltered by chalky hills with picturesque 18th- to 19th-century cottages set back on each side of the beck in its grassy hollow, this is a village not to be missed. St Edith's Church enjoys a lofty location and has a tall recessed stone spire set above the tower. With its hammerbeam roof, it is said to be one of Sir Tatton Sykes' best restorations.

WHAT TO LOOK OUT FOR

Note the straw sculptures of animals on Burnby Lane. There are fine views from numerous points – look out for York Minster, a hilltop church at Holme on Spalding Moor, and even Drax Power Station. Also views of wold dales from Nunburnholme Wold and lynchets (terraces) on steeper slopes around Givendale, Londesborough and Nunburnholme. Wooded areas seasonally show a profusion of bluebells, wood anemone and some wild garlic. In the chalky areas you may see common spotted orchids, clustered bellflower and autumn gentian. Millington Wood Nature Reserve, a wold ash woodland, has a good variety of flowering plants. Also, see if you can spot, somewhere along the route but not in a churchyard, a headstone where a notable dairy cow is interred.

PONTEFRACT–RICHMOND

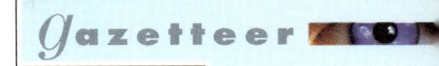

▶ This historic market town is famous for its liquorice confectionery known as Pontefract cakes. Pontefract Castle, now a ruin and open to the public, featured in Shakespeare's *Richard II*, called Pomfret. Pontefract Museum in Salter Row displays the town's history and its industries, especially glass-blowing and confectionery.

▶ The largest village in Swaledale, Reeth lies near the confluence of the rivers Swale and Arkle, surrounded by the Pennine range. The mining of lead, started by the Romans, formed the staple industry for many years. Following its decline the emphasis fell on agriculture. The Folk Museum depicts life and traditions in Swaledale.

▶ This pretty market town, the capital of Richmondshire, is dominated by its castle and centred around its cobbled market square. Buildings such as the town hall (1756) and The King's Head hotel in the market place reflect the prosperity of the town in this period, which came from its thriving market trade, when the town served an area stretching into Lancashire. The Georgian theatre, built in 1788, is the oldest in England and as well as a programme of performances it also houses a museum with collections of playbills, painted scenery and model theatres. St Mary's Church, in existence since at least 1135, contains much medieval work.

Alan Rufus, 1st Earl of Richmond, built the original Norman castle here in 1071. The site, high up on a rocky promontory, with the River Swale passing below, was well chosen for defending the town.

PONTEFRACT
WEST YORKSHIRE. TOWN ON A645, 12 MILES (19KM) SE OF LEEDS

REETH
NORTH YORKSHIRE. VILLAGE ON B6270, 9 MILES (14KM) W OF RICHMOND

RICHMOND
NORTH YORKSHIRE. TOWN ON A6108, 11 MILES (18KM) SW OF DARLINGTON

Once a stronghold against all-comers, the substantial ruins of Richmond Castle still look daunting as they perch high above the River Swale

gazetteer

RICHMOND—RIEVAULX ABBEY

Georgian Theatre Royal
VICTORIA ROAD
TEL: 01748 823710

▶ Built in 1778, this is the oldest theatre in the United Kingdom still in its original form and still being used for live theatre. Having closed in 1848, it was restored and re-opened in 1962. The audience now watch the actors from the original gallery, boxes and pit. The museum contains old playbills and photographs, and the oldest complete set of painted scenery in the country.

Open Apr–Oct, daily.

Green Howards Museum
TRINITY CHURCH SQUARE,
MARKET PLACE
TEL: 01748 822133

▶ This award-winning museum traces the military history of the Green Howards from the late-17th century onwards. The exhibits include uniforms, weapons, medals and a special Victoria Cross exhibition. Regimental and civic plate is also displayed.

Open Feb–Nov, most days.

Richmond Castle
TEL: 01748 822493

▶ Commanding a powerful position on the banks of the River Swale, this mighty fortress was never put to the test, for Richmond has never seen military action. Its location is superb, with steep cliffs protecting one side, and thick walls defending the other sides.

The Normans started constructing a castle here in the 1080s, and it is thought that Scolland's Hall, a fine two-storeyed hall with typical round-headed windows, is one of the earliest stone-built halls in England. The towers at Richmond have romantic names: Robin Hood Tower, now in ruins, is said to have been the prison of William the Lion, King of Scotland; the Gold Hole Tower may have a poetic ring to its name, but it was actually the latrine tower, complete with pits at its base, spanned by an interesting 11th-century arch. By far the largest building of the entire complex is the keep. It started life as a gatehouse in the 11th century, but in the mid-12th century it was extended upwards to a height of 100 feet (30m). Straight flights of stairs ran between the floors, rather than the traditional spiral stairways. Richmond Castle is now in the care of English Heritage.

Open all year daily. Closed 24–26 Dec & 1 Jan.

RIEVAULX ABBEY
NORTH YORKSHIRE. 2 MILES (3KM) W OF HELMSLEY ON MINOR ROAD OFF B1257
TEL: 01439 798228

▶ The site for this magnificent abbey (English Heritage) was given to a band of 12 Cistercian monks in 1131. Building began in about 1132 and most was completed by the end of the 12th century. The abbey was extremely prosperous, and under its third abbot, Aelred (1147–67), there were 140 monks and over 500 lay brothers. During the 15th century parts of the abbey were taken down as numbers fell, and by the time of the Dissolution there were only 22 monks left.

Surrounded by wooded hills, this site in the Rye Valley is one of the most beautiful in England. The remains of the high church and monastic buildings are extensive, and the choir is a notable example

RIEVAULX TERRACE & TEMPLES–RIPLEY

gazetteer

The substantial remains of Rievaulx Abbey

of a 13th-century work. The nave, which dates back to 1135, is the earliest large Cistercian nave in Britain.

Open all year, daily. Closed 24–26 Dec & 1 Jan.

▶ This curved terrace (National Trust), half a mile long, overlooks the abbey, with views of Ryedale and the Hambleton Hills. It has two mock-Greek temples, one built for hunting parties, the other for quiet contemplation. There are also remarkable frescoes by Borgnis, and an exhibition on English landscape design.

Open Apr–Oct, daily. There is no access to the abbey from the terrace.

▶ This charming estate village adjoining Ripley Castle was rebuilt by Sir William Amcotts Ingilby in the style of a village he had seen during his travels in Alsace-Lorraine. Ripley Castle, which has been home of the Ingilbys for over 600 years, is now open to the public along with its deer park and gardens.

▶ Ripley Castle, home to the Ingilby family since 1320, stands in a delightful estate with a deer park, lake and walled gardens. The castle has a rich history and a fine collection of Royalist armour is housed in the 1555 tower. Friendly, informative tours bring the passage of time to life. There are also walled gardens, tropical hot houses, woodland walks, pleasure grounds and the National Hyacinth collection in spring. Special events are held during the summer months.

Castle open Apr–Oct, certain days.

RIEVAULX TERRACE & TEMPLES

NORTH YORKSHIRE. 2 MILES (3KM) NW OF HELMSLEY OFF B1257
TEL: 01439 798340

RIPLEY

NORTH YORKSHIRE. VILLAGE ON A61, 3 MILES (5KM) N OF HARROGATE

Ripley Castle

OFF A61, HARROGATE TO RIPON RD.
TEL: 01423 770152

67

gazetteer

RIPON

The splendid west front of Ripon Cathedral

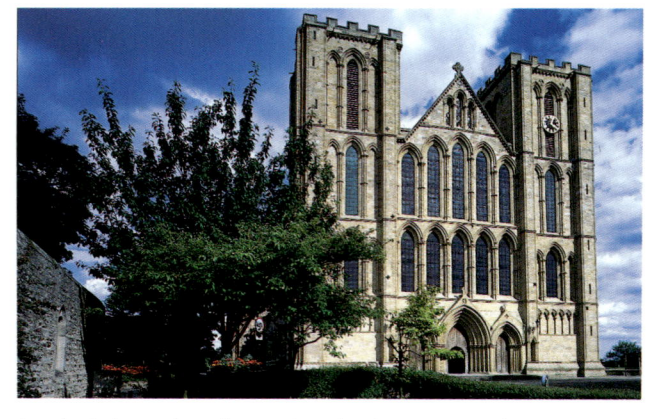

RIPON
NORTH YORKSHIRE. CITY ON A61, 10 MILES (16KM) N OF HARROGATE

▶ A cathedral city whose history dates back to AD 886 when it was granted a charter by Alfred the Great, Ripon's focal point is now the large market place with its 90ft (27m) obelisk. This is surrounded by Georgian and medieval buildings including the town hall, completed in 1801, and the 14th-century half-timbered Wakeman's House. The Ripon Prison and Police Museum, built as a House of Correction in 1686, is in St Marygate. From the obelisk the city's official hornblower sounds the 'Setting of the Watch' every evening at 9pm to assure everyone that they are in safekeeping for the night – a ritual maintained without fail for over 1,100 years.

Ripon Cathedral dates from 672, contains many architectural styles, in particular Gothic, from the 12th to the 16th centuries, has some of the highest vaults and yet is one of the smallest cathedrals in Britain. It has an Anglo-Saxon crypt and treasury with a large collection of silver and silvergilt ecclesiastical treasures.

Fountains Abbey & Studley Royal
4M (6.5KM) W OFF B6265
TEL: 01765 608888

▶ Founded by Cistercian monks in 1132, Fountains Abbey (National Trust) is the largest monastic ruin in Britain. It was acquired by William Aislabie in 1768, and became the focal point of his landscaped gardens at Studley. These include formal water gardens, ornamental temples, follies and magnificent views. They are bordered by a lake and 400 acres (162ha) of deer park. Other interesting features include Fountains Hall, built between 1598 and 1611 using the stone from the abbey ruins.

Open all year, most days. Closed 24–25 Dec.

Ripon Prison & Police Museum
ST MARYGATE
TEL: 01765 690799

▶ This early 19th-century prison is now a museum, housing documents, prints and memorabilia depicting the history of Law and Order and the Penal system in Ripon over the last 100 years.

Open Apr–Oct, afternoons.

Gazetteer

▶ This small town clings to a steep cliff overlooking the North Sea. Cobbled slopes, flights of steps and narrow alleyways weave between the terraces and groups of small stone cottages with pink pantiled roofs. Smuggling was a profitable activity here in the 18th and 19th centuries and The Smuggling Experience, open during the summer season, captures the era well.

ROBIN HOOD'S BAY
NORTH YORKSHIRE. SMALL TOWN ON B1447, 5 MILES (8KM) SE OF WHITBY

▶ The walls of the south and north transepts still stand to their full height in this 12th-century Cistercian abbey, now in the care of English Heritage, providing a dramatic sight for the visitor. There is also a fine gatehouse to the north-west.
Open Apr–Oct, daily.

ROCHE ABBEY
SOUTH YORKSHIRE. 1½ MILES (2.5KM) S OF MALTBY OFF A634
TEL: 01709 812739

▶ Rotherham lies where the rivers Rother and Don meet. The Romans worked iron here and built a fort on the south bank of the Don at Templeborough. The site was excavated over 100 years ago and finds from this and subsequent digs can be seen at Clifton Park Museum.

The town grew up around heavy industries, mining and engineering, much of which has now declined, although there has been some considerable investment in Rotherham's steel production. At the centre of the town is the Parish Church of All Saints which dates from the 15th century, although there is evidence of an earlier Saxon church on the site. The Chapel of Our Lady on Rotherham Bridge was also built at around the same time and, now renovated and re-consecrated, it is one of the few remaining bridge chapels in the country.

Clifton Park Museum in Clifton House contains a fine collection of locally made Rockingham Pottery. The interior of Clifton House has changed little since it was built in 1783 for Rotherham ironmaster Joshua Walker.

ROTHERHAM
SOUTH YORKSHIRE. TOWN OFF M1, 6 MILES (10KM) NE OF SHEFFIELD

▶ The gallery hosts a continuous programme of temporary exhibitions covering a wide range of historic and artistic subjects. The annual programme is drawn together from a variety of sources; some exhibitions are shown as part of a national tour, others are drawn from the museum's own collections or showcase the talents of local people.
Open all year, most days.

Art Gallery
WALKER PLACE. FOLLOW BROWN TOURIST INFORMATION SIGNS FROM MAIN ROADS
TEL: 01709 382121 EXT 3624/3635

▶ Housed in a mansion designed by John Carr, the museum is noted for its collection of Rockingham china. Other attractions include the 18th-century rooms, family portraits, the period kitchen, Victoriana, natural history displays, geology and glassware. There is a regular programme of temporary exhibitions.
Open all year, most days. Closed Xmas & New Year.

Museum
CLIFTON PARK, CLIFTON LN. FOLLOW DIRECTIONS TO INNER RING ROAD
TEL: 01709 382121 EXT 3628/3635

gazetteer

SALTAIRE—SCARBOROUGH

SALTAIRE
WEST YORKSHIRE. TOWN OFF A650, JUST W OF SHIPLEY

▶ This model town is named after its founder, Sir Titus Salt, the successful Victorian industrialist who in 1850 decided to move his mohair and alpaca factory out from the smoke of Bradford to a site on the River Aire, close to the Yorkshire Dales. In addition to the houses, Salt provided schools, a hospital, churches, almshouses, baths, a steam laundry and a park. Many of the buildings are well preserved and the town has become a popular tourist attraction. Salt's Mill houses a permanent exhibition of the works of David Hockney.

Reed Organ & Harmonium Museum
VICTORIA HALL, VICTORIA ROAD
TEL: 01274 585601
AFTER 6PM

▶ Europe's first reed organ museum contains a collection of 70 models. The smallest is no bigger than a family bible and the largest, which belonged to Dr Marmaduke P Conway when he was organist at Ely Cathedral, has three manuals and pedals. If you are a player, you may have the chance to try some of the instruments. There are also harmoniums on display which have featured on television and radio.
  Open all year, most days. Closed 2 wks Xmas.

SCARBOROUGH
NORTH YORKSHIRE. TOWN ON A170, 35 MILES (56KM) NE OF YORK

▶ The two bays and the town of Scarborough are dominated by Castle Hill, a flat-topped promontory upon which the gaunt remains of Scarborough Castle stand. Visitors to this traditional seaside resort could not fail to be impressed by the panoramic setting of the cliffs and bays here. It was Scarborough's spring water, however, discovered in 1626 by Mrs Tomazyn Farrer, that first drew the crowds, and the coming of the railway from York in 1846 really established Scarborough as a resort. It still retains a very traditional feel, with Regency and Victorian buildings, bandstands and gardens, donkey rides and Punch and Judy tents. The Spa, or 'Spaw House', originally built in 1700 and rebuilt in 1877, is now a huge entertainment and conference complex, housing the grand hall, a ballroom, a theatre and numerous shops and cafés.
  Scarborough Castle dates from the 12th century and in its time was twice besieged by Parliamentarian forces, in 1643 and 1648. The Quaker George Fox was imprisoned here in 1665. In the Civil War Scarborough was ultimately the only Royalist port on the east coast and it was not until 1645 that the castle surrendered to Parliament. Today staged battles in the summer holiday season are a popular attraction for tourists.
  There are visible remains of a Roman signal station on Castle Hill, believed to have been built in AD 370 as a look-out post. The port consists of three piers enclosing an outer and inner harbour. Up to 1950 the main industry was fishing but since then the commercial traffic of the port has increased. Anne Brontë, who died aged 28 on 28 May 1849, is buried in the churchyard of the Church of St Mary.

SCARBOROUGH

gazetteer

▶ Unlike most medieval castles, Scarborough saw action in World War I, when shells from German battleships damaged its walls. Historical records indicate that this was by no means the first time that the castle has come under attack, and several English kings received bills for repairs, from Henry II to James I.

The rocky headland on which the castle was built had been an important site for hundreds of years before the Normans came, the cliffs providing a natural defence which was further strengthened by curtain walls. The keep, now in ruins, was built by Henry II on the site of an earlier tower. It was originally 100 feet (30m) high, and had walls that were up to 12 feet (3.7m) thick. There was also a forebuilding that has not survived.

Scarborough was also attacked in 1536 during the 'Pilgrimage of Grace', a rebellion against Henry VIII which protested against issues such as the Dissolution of the Monasteries, the Reformation and a whole host of economic grievances. The rebellion, mainly in the north, was led by Robert Ashe. Henry VIII agreed to listen to the complaints of the leaders, but as soon as the rebels began to disband, he had 230 of them, including Ashe, executed.

Open Apr–Oct, daily; Nov–Mar most days. Closed 24–26 Dec & 1 Jan.

Scarborough Castle
Tel: 01723 372451

Old cottages line the hills overlooking Scarborough harbour, above

gazetteer

SELBY–SHEFFIELD

Selby abbey stands, surrounded by lawns, in the attractive little market place at the heart of the town

SELBY
NORTH YORKSHIRE. TOWN ON A19, 13 MILES (21KM) S OF YORK

▶ The town, dominated by its famous abbey church, is an important local market and shopping centre and a thriving port on the River Ouse. Many of the buildings date from the 19th century when the town expanded with the coming of the railway. But its history goes back to the 11th century and the founding of Selby abbey by a monk of Auxerre in France who, following a vision, came to England. The present church was started by Hugh de Lacy in 1100. Building went slowly and was not finally completed until the 14th century.

SETTLE
NORTH YORKSHIRE. TOWN OFF A65, 13 MILES (21KM) NW OF SKIPTON

▶ Lying at the start of the scenic Settle to Carlisle Railway line, this small market town is an attractive tourist destination and a busy working town. It has many 17th-century buildings, including The Folly, on Kirkgate, which has unusual corner windows. Overlooking the market square is an attractive row of arcaded shops known as the Shambles. Near by is Ye Olde Naked Man Café which kept the name of the inn previously on the site. The Museum of North Craven Life illustrates aspects of local history and archaeology.

SHEFFIELD
SOUTH YORKSHIRE. CITY OFF M1, 144 MILES (232KM) NW OF LONDON

▶ Sheffield is Britain's fifth largest city with a population of 520,000, famous for its manufacture of steel and cutlery. It sits in the southern foothills of the Pennines on the River Don in a surrounding landscape predominantly of valleys and trees, and is very much an industrial city in a country setting.

SHEFFIELD

gazetteer

By the 17th century this small town had already acquired a reputation for its knives and tools, exploiting the fast-flowing rivers which turned grindstones and hammers. In the second half of the 17th century Sheffield also began to make its own steel. Although of a much later period, the only visible reminder today of Sheffield's first steel-making technology is the cementation furnace preserved at Hoyle Street in the Netherhope district of the city.

During the Industrial Revolution steel, cutlery and tool production expanded enormously. Benjamin Huntsman's invention in 1742 of a way to make a superior form of steel, crucible steel, transformed steel-making processes. By 1850 Sheffield was producing 90 per cent of Britain's steel. In 1913 Harry Brearley accidentally discovered stainless steel as he sought to prevent the rusting of barrels in Lee Enfield rifles. He was quick to see the commercial potential of his discovery and it was soon used for cutlery, engineering and surgical instruments.

Although Sheffield's metal-manufacturing industries contracted in terms of employment during the post-war era, the output of steel, cutting edges and cutlery has never been higher. To maintain employment levels the city has diversified into the service sector which now employs over 70 per cent of the workforce.

Along the central corridor from Castlegate in the north of the city to Moorfoot in the south are the city's main shopping areas. The Moor and Fargate are pedestrianised and Orchard Square, in the heart of

Colourful flowerbeds in Sheffield's pedestrianised shopping areas

gazetteer

SHEFFIELD

the city centre, now a courtyard-style shopping precinct was once a clutter of small workshops. Here John Brown, inventor of the railway buffer and pioneer manufacturer of railway lines and armour plate, began his career. Brown's achievements are commemorated by the figure of Elsie the buffer girl, who appears each quarter hour on the square's tower clock.

Sheffield has few early buildings of note. Those datting from the 19th century include the Cutlers' Hall with its Grecian façade, and there are some Georgian houses close by in Paradise Square. At Cutlers' Hall, visitors can see the Norfolk Knife which was two years in the making and a top prize-winner for its unsurpassed craftsmanship at the 1851 Great Exhibition. Kelham Island Industrial Museum, on Alma Street, contains a 10-ton bomb and the 400-ton working River Don Engine.

Sheffield's Crucible Theatre is probably best known as the venue of the annual World Snooker Championship, but is also a leading repertory theatre.

Bishops House
MEERSBROOK PARK, NORTON LEES LN. S OF SHEFFIELD, ON A61 CHESTERFIELD ROAD
TEL: 0114 255 7701

▶ This 15th- and 16th-century yeoman's house has been restored and opened as a museum of local and social history. Several rooms have been furnished and there are displays of life in Tudor and Stuart times, as well as a range of temporary exhibitions.

Open all year, most days. Closed Xmas & New Year.

City Museum & Mappin Art Gallery
WESTON PARK. ON A57
TEL: 0114 276 8588

▶ The museum houses exhibits on regional geology, natural history and archaeology, especially from the Peak District. There is a particularly splendid display of cutlery and Sheffield plate, for which the city is famous, among exhibits on other local industries such as ceramics, clocks, watches and sundials. The Mappin Art Gallery, housed in a Victorian Listed building, organises a programme of temporary exhibitions and special events with emphasis on contemporary art and Victorian paintings.

Open all year, most days. Closed 23 Dec–1 Jan.

Kelham Island Industrial Museum
ALMA ST. ½ MILE (1KM) NW OF CITY CENTRE, TAKE A61 N TO WEST BAR
TEL: 0114 272 2106

▶ The museum tells the story of Sheffield, its industry and life. The mighty River Don Engine, the most powerful working steam engine in Europe, can be seen 'in steam'. There are reconstructed workshops, a working cutler and craftspeople demonstrating traditional 'made in Sheffield' skills showing how the people of Sheffield lived and worked in days gone by. During the year Kelham Island stages events, displays and temporary exhibitions for the additional interest of visitors, culminating in the annual Christmas Victorian Market.

Open all year, most days.

SHIPLEY—SKIPTON

gazetteer

▶ Shipley has several notable houses including one dated 1593, with mullioned windows and gargoyles. The town is the home of the World of Sooty exhibition.

▶ Known as 'the gateway to the Dales', Skipton's origins can be traced to the 7th century when Anglian farmers called it 'Sheeptown'. The Normans built the first castle here in the 12th century, and established the markets and fairs which have carried on here ever since, in the wide cobbled market place. The town is dominated by Skipton Castle, standing behind the 14th-century Church of the Holy Trinity, and 200 feet (60m) above Eller Beck. The Leeds to Liverpool Canal runs through Skipton offering opportunities for tow-path walks and boat trips.

▶ Folk history, archaeology, geology, costumes, lead mining – this small museum, which is crammed full of curios, is bound to have something of interest for everyone.
   Open all year, most days.

▶ Skipton is one of the most complete and well-preserved medieval castles in England. Some of the castle dates from the 1650s when it was rebuilt after being partially damaged following the Civil War. However, the original castle was erected in Norman times, and the gateway with its Norman arch still exists. The castle became the home of the Clifford family in 1310 and remained so until 1676. Entrance to the castle is through a massive round-towered gateway with the family motto *Desormais* (henceforth) carved above it. The castle has an enormous banqueting hall, a series of kitchens, a beautiful Tudor

SHIPLEY
WEST YORKSHIRE. TOWN ON A657, 3 MILES (5KM) NW OF BRADFORD

SKIPTON
NORTH YORKSHIRE. TOWN OFF A629, 16 MILES (26KM) NW OF BRADFORD

Craven Museum
TOWN HALL, HIGH ST
TEL: 01756 706407

Skipton Castle
TEL: 01756 792442

Skipton Castle has been altered greatly over the centuries

gazetteer

STAITHES

NORTH YORKSHIRE. VILLAGE ON A174, 9 MILES (14KM) NW OF WHITBY

STOKESLEY

NORTH YORKSHIRE. SMALL TOWN OFF THE A172, 8 MILES (13KM) S OF MIDDLESBROUGH

SUTTON PARK

NORTH YORKSHIRE. ON B1363.
TEL: 01347 810249

RIVER SWALE

The River Swale, which runs through Reeth and Richmond, is a tributary of the Ure. Despite its puicturesque appearance, the Swale is one of the most ferocious rivers in England. Swaledale is patterned with drystone walls.

courtyard with an ancient yew tree and an unusual 19th-century room decorated with exotic shells brought back by George Clifford, the 3rd Earl of Cumberland, from his sea voyages. The main buildings inside the walls are surrounded by well-kept lawns and cobblestones. Conduit Court is especially attractive with its ancient yew tree. Illustrated tour sheets are available in English, French, German, Dutch, Italian, Spanish, Japanese and Esperanto.

Open all year, daily. Closed 25 Dec.

▶ This village, a favourite with artists, is set on the cliffs near Whitby. The modern part is set up on the main road, while the older village, from which cars are restricted, lies below the cliff. The old fishing community, with the cottages jumbled around the tiny harbour, is where Captain Cook was apprenticed to a grocer.

▶ The town lies on the River Leven and there are various bridges over the river in the town; the narrow packhorse bridge has low walls allowing animals carrying heavy packs to cross the water. Stokesly was home to Jane Pace, the first white woman to settle in Victoria, Australia, in 1836.

▶ The early Georgian house contains fine furniture, paintings and porcelain. The grounds have superb, award-winning terraced gardens, a lily pond, walled-in pond garden and a Georgian ice house. There are also delightful woodland walks as well as spaces for caravans.

Gardens open Etr–Oct, daily. House open Etr Sun & Mon and all BH Sun & Mon.

Fishing cobles in the tiny harbour at Staithes

Picnic site: Sutton Bank

It is a short step from the car park and picnic site at Sutton Bank, 6 miles (10km) east of Thirsk on the edge of the Hambleton Hills in the North York Moors National Park, to what the popular author and vet James Herriot once described as the finest view in England.

HOW TO GET THERE

Take the A170 Pickering to Scarborough road from Thirsk and drive east, crossing the A19 and passing through Sutton-under-Whitestonecliffe. Sutton Bank is approached by a very steep (1-in-4 gradient) hairpin bend, and the entrance to the car park and picnic site is on the left at the top.

FACILITIES

Pay-and-display parking. National Park Visitor Centre with a shop and interesting interpretive displays (open from April to the end of October).
Refreshment facilities for 40 people.
Toilets, with provision made for people with disabilities.

THE SITE

Sutton Bank is notorious for its formidable 1-in-4 hairpin road, which climbs 630 feet (180m) in 1 mile (1.5km), from the flat pastures of the Vale of Mowbray to the limestone uplands of the Hambleton Hills.

The view west from Sutton Bank

Picnic site

SUTTON BANK

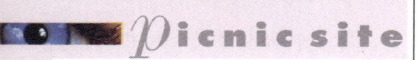

But the reward is what former local resident James Herriot described as the finest view in England. The view from Sutton Bank can extend as far as 90 miles (149km) in exceptionally clear conditions. In any weather, the stunning panorama looking south to the crags of Roulston Scar, with the outlying tree-capped Hood Hill and the Vale of York beyond, or the view east over the Vale of Mowbray to the distant blue line of the Pennines, is breathtaking. The circular, glacier-formed Gormire Lake, embowered in woodland, adds foreground interest at the foot of the escarpment, and a viewing plaque aids the view.

WALKS FROM THE VIEW

The North York Moors National Park authority has prepared a number of easy, waymarked, family-length walks from the site. Among these are the 3-mile (5km) stroll to the south to inspect the famous Kilburn White Horse, the only one in the north of England, which was carved out of limestone on the south-facing scarp of Roulston Scar by a local schoolmaster in 1857.

Other walks include an excursion along the Hambleton Drove Road, now followed by the Cleveland Way long-distance path, along which Scottish cattle were driven to English markets; and the descent to Gormire Lake through the Yorkshire Wildlife Trusts's beautiful mixed woodland nature reserve of Garbutt Wood, where primroses and bluebells bloom in spring.

CLOSE BY

The Herriot industry has made an impact on Thirsk and the countryside around because the late author and vet, whose real name was Alfred Whight,

The White Horse of Kilburn

practised in this busy little market town.

Also near at hand is the lovely little market town of Helmsley, with its imposing castle dating from 1186, and the romantic ruins of Rievaulx and Byland abbeys.

THIRSK–TODMORDEN

▶ Thirsk was a major stopping point in the days of stage coaches, and many of the traditional coaching inns can still be seen around the cobbled market square. The splendid Parish Church of St Mary is known as the 'cathedral of the north'. The town has a racecourse and many horses are stabled here.

▶ A magnificent 14th-century gatehouse and the ruins of the church and other buildings survive from the Augustinian abbey, founded in 1139. The gate is approached across a dry moat, spanned by a long bridge with arcaded walls and circular towers. Thornton Abbey is in the care of English Heritage.
   Open all year, daily.

▶ This attractive village, at one end of the scenic North Yorkshire Moors Railway, takes its shape from the Middle Ages but its character from later times. There are many Georgian houses as well as pretty, stone thatched cottages, and a rustic bridge which spans Thornton Beck.

▶ The market town grew after the Rochdale Canal was built and because of this link to Lancashire, cotton rather than wool was the predominant industry here. Todmorden Hall dates from the 17th century. With the new-found wealth from textiles, many of the town's older buildings were replaced in the 19th century and public buildings were erected.

THIRSK
NORTH YORKSHIRE. TOWN OFF A618, 8 MILES (13KM) SE OF NORTHALLERTON

THORNTON ABBEY
EAST RIDING OF YORKSHIRE
TEL: 01469 40357

THORNTON DALE
NORTH YORKSHIRE. VILLAGE ON A170, 3 MILES (5KM) E OF PICKERING

TODMORDEN
WEST YORKSHIRE. TOWN ON A6033, 8 MILES (12KM) NE OF ROCHDALE

Picturesque Thornton Dale

gazetteer

WAKEFIELD

WAKEFIELD
WEST YORKSHIRE. CITY OFF M1, 8 MILES (13KM) S OF LEEDS

Above, St Mary's Chantry Chapel on Wakefield Bridge

Opposite, West Burton nestles in a rich green valley

▶ The cathedral city of Wakefield prospered for many years as an inland grain and cloth port. The old town, built on a hill overlooking the River Calder, grew up around the crossroads of the main streets – Westgate, Northgate and Kirkgate.

At the very centre of the town is the Cathedral of All Saints, built in the 13th century, whose spire dominates the skyline and at 247 feet (75m) high is the tallest in Yorkshire. The cathedral is now surrounded by pedestrianised shopping areas leading to the traditional outdoor market, market halls and the Ridings shopping centre.

The city's museum has a fine collection of exotic birds and animals from South America, and local archaeological finds dating back 300 years. The art gallery includes some works by two Yorkshire sculptors, Barbara Hepworth and Henry Moore.

St Mary's Chantry Chapel, built in the 14th century on the old Wakefield Bridge spanning the River Calder, is the sole survivor of four chapels built in Wakefield as resting places for travellers. Wakefield Bridge was built in the early 1340s.

The Theatre Royal and Opera House were designed by the renowned Edwardian architect Frank Matcham.

WAKEFIELD—WETHERBY

gazetteer

- Wakefield was home to two of Britain's greatest modern sculptors – Barbara Hepworth and Henry Moore. The art gallery, which has an important collection of 20th-century paintings and sculptures, has a special room devoted to these two local artists. There are frequent temporary exhibitions of both modern and earlier works covering all aspects of art and crafts.
  Open all year, daily. Closed Xmas & New Year.

- Wakefield Museum is full of objects and images which depict Wakefield's long and complex history – from flint axes and Roman pottery to steam trains and plastic tea cups. The museum also houses the exotic and eccentric natural history collections of the Victorian explorer Charles Waterton. The are also temporary exhibitions covering a wide range, from wildlife photography to platform shoes.
  Open all year, daily. Closed Xmas, New Year & BH.

- The village is built around a large, central green with a distinctive pyramidical market cross dating from 1820 when a large weekly market was held on the green. Mill Force waterfall is best viewed from the little packhorse bridge leading to a footpath to the fells.

- This old coaching town is situated on the former Great North Road, with a market and racecourse. The town is wholly north of the winding Wharfe, and the riverside is a pleasant recreation area. See the Shambles of 1811 and the Town Hall, built in 1845.

Wakefield Art Gallery
WENTWORTH TER
TEL: 01924 305796

Wakefield Museum
WOOD ST
TEL: 01924 295351

WEST BURTON
NORTH YORKSHIRE. VILLAGE ON B6160, 1 MILE (2KM) SE OF AYSGARTH

WETHERBY
WEST YORKSHIRE. SMALL TOWN OFF A1, 12 MILES (23KM) SE OF BOROUGHBRIDGE

RIVER WHARFE
Wharfedale is the longest and one of the most spectacular of the Yorkshire dales, dominated by Great Scar limestone. The river begins almost as a moorland stream high on Cam Fell, and its peat-coloured water runs broad and shallow, capable of rising at great speed, through mid-Wharfedale.

gazetteer

WHITBY

Whitby's large harbour is at the heart of the town

WHITBY
NORTH YORKSHIRE. TOWN ON A171, 17 MILES (27KM) NW OF SCARBOROUGH

Whitby Abbey
ON CLIFFTOP E OF WHITBY TOWN CENTRE
TEL: 01947 603568

Whitby Museum
PANNETT PARK
TEL: 01947 602908

▶ Situated at the mouth of the River Esk, Whitby is a bustling fishing port and seaside resort on the east coast. Captain James Cook sailed from Whitby in the *Endeavour* in 1768, and as a young man lodged in the town with John Walker, a local ship owner. His house in Grape Street is now the Captain Cook Memorial Museum.

The attractive harbour has two lighthouses at its entrance, dating from 1835 and 1855. The West Lighthouse is open to the public in summer. On the cliffs high above the town are the jagged sandstone ruins of Whitby Abbey and 12th-century St Mary's Church, reached by 199 steps. The first abbey was founded by St Hilda in AD 657 on land given by the King of Northumbria. Later the Danes destroyed it and it was rebuilt by the Normans. In the 7th century the abbey was the home of Caedmon, the first English Christian poet and a cross commemorating him stands in St Mary's churchyard. The ruins that stand today are 13th century.

Abraham 'Bram' Stoker set three chapters of his novel *Dracula* around Whitby and a Dracula Trail can be followed around the town.

▶ Dominating the skyline above the fishing port of Whitby are the ruins of the 13th-century Benedictine abbey (English Heritage). The stone abbey was erected on the site of the wooden abbey of St Hilda, which was built in 657. It was badly damaged during World War I when two German battleships shelled the town.

Open all year, daily. Closed 24–26 Dec & 1 Jan.

▶ This charming museum is packed full of fascinating exhibits relating to Whitby's history. There are important collections of fossils, ship models, marine reptile skeletons and Whitby jet jewellery, along with Captain Cook material and relics of the whaling industry. Bygones, costumes, and local archaeology are also displayed.

Open all year, daily.

YORK

gazetteer

Few cities look as completely medieval as York. It began life as a fortress, built in AD 71 by the Roman 9th Legion and grew into an important city known as *Eboracum*.

The Vikings gave York its name, derived from Jorvik, during their brief but flourishing reign. Jorvik Viking Centre is built on the site of Viking remains discovered by archaeologists beneath Coppergate, and provides a vivid description of Viking-age York.

Norman rule lasted longer and the Normans made the city a vital centre of government, commerce and religion for the north, preparing the city well for its important role in the reigns of the Plantaganet kings. In 1485, when this era ended and the Tudor age began, York was already at its zenith.

The pride of York is its magnificent minster which towers over the whole city. It contains England's greatest concentration of medieval stained glass, the two most famous windows being the 'Five Sisters' in the north transept, and the great east window which covers 2,000 square feet (186sq m), thought to be the largest area of medieval coloured glass in the world. The minster took 250 years to build and was completed and consecrated in 1472.

Treasurers' House was the residence for Treasurers of the Minster until 1547. It now belongs to the National Trust and has a fine collection of period furnishings. The medieval centre of the city is

YORK

NORTH YORKSHIRE. CITY OFF A64, 212 MILES (341KM) N OF LONDON

York Minster, one of England's best examples of Gothic architecture

gazetteer

YORK

reached through the four great Bars in the city walls, Micklegate, Bootham, Monk and Walmgate Bars. A walk around the walls, which were built during the reign of Henry II (1216–72) is a good introduction to the city.

In the Middle Ages York was an important wool-trading centre and fine cloth was woven here. The prosperity that this trade brought allowed other trades and craftspeople to thrive in the city, such as goldsmiths, silversmiths, saddlers, barbers, butchers and shoemakers. They lived and worked in the areas known as Stonegate, Goodramgate and the Shambles, the narrow old butchers' quarter, all still very medieval in appearance. Today these areas have an excellent range of smart shops, including bookshops and interesting antique and jewellery specialists.

York's splendid Georgian Mansion House was built between 1725 and 1730, and has the distinction of being the only house in England today which is used solely as the official private residence for a Lord Mayor during his term in office.

The Industrial Revolution for the most part passed York by, but the city did become a great railway centre when the first railway line to York opened in 1839. The city has a splendid station and the station hotel, The Royal York, has also been restored to its original grandeur. The National Railway Museum is located in York.

Besides the railways, the other major employer in York has for many years been the confectionery trade. Rowntree's, Terry's, and Craven's all began here and the industry continues to thrive on the outskirts of the city centre.

The Shambles in York, a short narrow street of almost perfectly preserved medieval buildings

The ARC
St Saviourgate
Tel: 01904 654324

▶ The ARC is a 'hands-on' experience of archaeology, enjoyed by visitors of all ages. It is housed in the beautifully restored medieval Church of St Saviour. Visitors can sift through the remains of centuries – bones, shell, pottery and much more. Piece together the lives of our ancestors, solve the puzzle of how to open a Viking padlock, decipher Viking-age writing or learn to make a Roman shoe. Real archaeologists are on hand to assist with your discoveries. A range of special events and exhibitions of archaeological interest are held throughout the year.

Open all year, most days. Closed 15 Dec–2 Jan.

YORK gazetteer

▶ Six hundred years of painting is covered in the City Art Gallery, from early Italian gold-ground panels to the art of the 20th century. Exceptional in its range and interest, the collection includes works by Parmigianino and Bellotto, Lely, Reynolds, Frith, Boudin, Lowry and Nash, and nudes by Etty. An outstanding collection of studio pottery can also bee seen. There is a varied and exciting programme of temporary exhibitions and event, a gallery shop and facilities for visitors with disabilities.

Open all year, daily. Closed Good Fri, 25–26 Dec & 1 Jan.

City Art Gallery
EXHIBITION SQUARE
TEL: 01904 551861

▶ Known as Clifford's Tower, after Roger de Clifford who was hung from the castle by chains, York Castle was built in 1086 by William the Conqueror as part of his campaign to subdue the Saxons. He built a large mound, topped with a wooden castle, on the banks of the River Ouse. In 1190 it was burned down when the Jews of York hid in it during the pogrom. Under the reign of King John it was rebuilt in stone and was completed in 1313. However, the castle cracked from top to bottom in 1360, as a result of part of the mound subsiding into the moat. From the end of the 15th century the tower was largely unused. Since 1825 Clifford's Tower has been part of the prison and is now looked after by English Heritage. The wall walk provides one of the best views of York.

Open all year, daily. Closed 24–26 Dec & 1 Jan.

Clifford's Tower
TOWER ST
TEL: 01904 646940

Originally constructed as the central keep of the castle, Clifford's Tower was built in the 13th century by Henry II

gazetteer

YORK

Fairfax House
CASTLEGATE. IN CITY CENTRE, CLOSE TO JORVIK CENTRE AND CLIFFORDS TOWER
TEL: 01904 655543

▶ An outstanding mid 18th-century house with a richly decorated interior, Fairfax House was acquired by the York Civic Trust in 1983 and restored. Prior to this it had been used as a cinema and a dance hall. The house contains fine examples of Georgian furniture, porcelain, paintings and clocks which form the Terry Collection. This collection was donated by Mr Noel Terry who was the great grandson of Joseph Terry the founder of the York-based confectionery business.

Open end Feb–1st week Jan, daily.

Friargate Museum
LOWER FRIARGATE. CITY CENTRE.
TEL: 01904 658775

▶ The award-winning Friargate – the most popular family museum in York – is celebrated for its role in bringing history to life. Over 70 life-size waxworks figures are exhibited in carefully reconstructed, realistic sets, showing scenes such as Drake and the Armada, The Dukes of York, the Crown Jewels, and a life-size Yeti or 'Abominable Snowman'.

Open all year, daily. Closed Jan & 25 Dec.

Guildhall
OFF CONEY ST
TEL: 01904 613161

▶ The hall dates from 1446 but in 1942 an air raid virtually destroyed the building. The present Guildhall was carefully restored as an exact replica and was re-opened in 1960. There is an interesting arch-braced roof decorated with colourful bosses and supported by 12 solid oak pillars. Although many of the windows in the Guildhall were unglazed until the 18th century, the west window contains stained glass from 1682, by a York craftsman, and there is also a superb, modern stained-glass window by Henry Harvey. This depicts the story of York through the ages. The Inner Chamber adjoining the hall has two secret doors and a passageway beneath the Guildhall to the river.

Open all year, most days. Closed Good Fri, Spring BH, 25–26 Dec & 1 Jan.

Jorvik Viking Centre
COPPERGATE
TEL: 01904 643211

▶ Between 1976 and 1981 archaeologists made some remarkable discoveries about Jorvik (the Viking name for York), during a dig in an area known as Coppergate. In 1984 the Viking Centre was opened over the site of the original excavations. The dig shed a totally new light on the Viking way of life and has revealed many details of tools, clothing, crafts and trade. The centre displays the archaeological remains – leather, textiles, metal objects and even timber buildings – in a detailed and vivid reconstruction. An audio-visual display, which explains exactly who the Vikings were, is followed by a journey in a 'time-car' which carries visitors through a 'time tunnel' from World War II back to Norman times and then to a full-scale reconstruction of 10th-century Coppergate. The busy street scene includes a crowded market, a river wharf with a fully-rigged sailing ship and a family at home. This is all made more authentic by voices speaking in Old

YORK gazetteer

Norse and even smells such as cooking, pigsties and rubbish. Finally the tour passes through a reconstruction of Coppergate during the dig of the 1970s. The visit ends in the Skipper Gallery which has a display of some of the 15,000 small objects found during the dig. The Jorvik Festival (February) features longship races, combat re-enactment, craft displays, a torchlit procession and boat burning ceremony.

Open all year, daily. Closed 25 Dec.

▶ The medieval guild hall of the powerful Merchant Adventurers' Company was built in 1357–61 and is one of the finest in Europe. The Great Hall, where the merchants conducted their business affairs, contains early furniture, one piece dating from the 13th century, paintings, silver, weights and measures, and other objects used by the merchants over the centuries. The building also has an undercroft where they cared for the poor, and a chapel.

Open all year, most days. Closed 10 days Xmas.

▶ Your ticket for the National Railway Museum will take you on a spectacular journey through the life and history of railways. The unique collection of engines, trains, paintings and photographs, supported by special exhibitions and interactive displays, are a celebration of a revolution that swept the world. Travel back to 1829 and be amazed by the inventive brilliance that made *Rocket* one of the world's most

Merchant Adventurers' Hall
Fossgate
Tel: 01904 654818

National Railway Museum
Leeman Rd
Tel: 01904 621261

Gleaming locomotives at the National Railway Museum

famous steam locomotives. Experience the golden age of steam travel from the platforms where station sound effects re-create the busy and exciting atmosphere of another era. Queen Victoria's luxurious royal carriage awaits you in all its regal splendour. Come face-to-face with the mighty *Mallard* – holder of the steam world speed record at 126 mph (203km), then speed right up-to-date in front of a life-size section of the Channel Tunnel and mock-up of *Eurostar*.

Open all year, daily. Closed 24–26 Dec.

St Williams College
5 COLLEGE ST. ADJACENT TO YORK MINSTER AT EAST END
TEL: 01904 637134

▶ St William's College, a 15th-century timber-framed building, housed chantry priests until 1549. It now contains York Minster's Visitor Centre and Conference Centre, shop and restaurant, and the medieval rooms are open to view when not being used for functions. Craft fairs are held most weekends.

Open all year to view medieval rooms subject to private bookings. Closed 24–26 Dec & Good Fri.

Treasurers' House
CHAPTER HOUSE
TEL: 01904 624247

▶ There has been a house on this site since Roman times and in the basement of this elegant 17th-century building is an exhibition of its history. The house was improved during the 18th century with the addition of a fine staircase. Restored between 1897 and 1930, it was left, with its fine furniture, to the National Trust.

Open end Mar–Oct, most days.

York Castle Museum
THE EYE OF YORK.
CITY CENTRE, NEXT TO CLIFFORD'S TOWER
TEL: 01904 653611

▶ Fascinating exhibits that bring memories to life, are imaginatively displayed here, through reconstructions of period rooms and two indoor streets, complete with cobbles, a Hansom cab and a park. The museum is housed in the city's prison and is based on an extensive collection of 'bygones' acquired at the beginning of the century. It was one of the first folk museums to display a huge range of everyday objects in an authentic scene. The Victorian street includes a pawnbroker, a tallow candle factory and a haberdasher's. There is even a reconstruction of the original sweet shop of the York chocolate manufacturer, Joseph Terry. An extensive collection of many other items ranging from musical instruments to costumes and a gallery of domestic gadgets from Victorian times to the 1960s (entitled 'Every Home Should Have One'), are further attractions to this remarkable museum. The museum also has one of Britain's finest collections of militaria; this includes a superb example of an Anglo-Saxon helmet – one

The original Terry's sweet shop is reconstructed in Castle Museum

YORK *gazetteer*

A Victorian street scene in York's Castle Museum

of only three known. A special exhibition called 'Seeing it Through' explores the life of York citizens during World War II.

Open all year, daily. Closed 25–26 Dec & 1 Jan.

▶ Deep in the heart of York, buried beneath Clifford Street, lies the North's most infamous museum of horror. Here, history is brought to life, and execution and torture are everyday events behind its doors.

Open all year, daily. Closed 25 Dec.

▶ It is believed that Edwin King of Northumbria built the first church on this site in 627. Since then both Saxons and Normans built cathedrals here, and parts of the latter survive in many places in the present structure. From 1220 to 1472 the present church was built to replace the Romanesque one. It is notable for its size – it is the largest medieval church north of the Alps – and for its wealth of stained glass, most of which is original to the building. Daily worship has been conducted on the site for 13 centuries.

Open all year, daily.

▶ One of the biggest and best model railways in Britain, York Model Railway has two very intricate railway layouts. The larger one is set in town and country landscapes. It comprises hundreds of buildings, about 5,500 tiny trees, over 2,000 lights and around 2,500 people and animals. As many as 14 trains can run in this model at the same

The York Dungeon
12 CLIFFORD ST
TEL: *01904 632599*

York Minster
OGLEFORTH
TEL: *01904 639347 & 647577*

York Model Railway
TEAROOM SQUARE, NEXT TO YORK STATION
TEL: *01904 63016*

89

gazetteer

YORK

time, including the Royal Train, the Orient Express, Inter City 125 and the latest freight and passenger trains. The second model is a much smaller layout and shows a typical German town at night, brightly lit by numerous tiny lights. There are push buttons for children, amid these detailed and accurate scale models.

Open all year, daily. Closed 25–26 Dec.

Yorkshire Air Museum & Allied Air Forces Memorial
HALIFAX WAY. FROM YORK TAKE A1079 (HULL RD) THEN IMMEDIATE RIGHT ON TO B1228. THE MUSEUM IS SIGNPOSTED ON RIGHT
TEL: 01904 608595

▶ The Yorkshire Air Museum is based on a part of the site of a typical World War II bomber base and its aim is to preserve it as a memorial to the Allied Air Force air and ground crews who served in World War II, and especially those who served in Yorkshire and Humberside. Interesting aircraft include one of the last of the RAF's Victor tankers, and the Halifax bomber Friday the 13th. It is also home to the Barnes Wallis Collection and displays of aviation artefacts and ephemera.

Open all year, daily.

Yorkshire Museum & Gardens
MUSEUM GARDENS
TEL: 01904 629745

▶ The winner of a European award, Yorkshire Museum – set in 10 acres (4ha) of botanical gardens – displays some of the finest Roman, Anglo-Saxon, Viking and medieval treasures ever discovered in Britain. The Middleham jewel, a fine example of English Gothic jewellery, is on display in the Medieval Gallery and, in the Roman Gallery, visitors can see a fine marble head of Constantine the Great, a re-created kitchen and many other artefacts. The Anglo-Saxon Gallery houses the magnificent, delicate silver-gilt Ormside bowl and the skilfully wrought Gilling sword. Part of York's Roman city walls runs through the gardens.

Open all year, daily. Closed 25–26 Dec & 1 Jan.

The York Story
ST MARY'S, CASTLEGATE. CITY CENTRE, NEAR JORVIK CENTRE
TEL: 01904 628632

▶ The exhibition traces the history of York over the last 1,000 years, helped by a large three-dimensional model of the city. A model of part of the building of a medieval church, showing the scaffolding and other construction techniques, is an unusual feature. There is a comprehensive audio-visual guide to the display of many notable pieces by modern artists and craftsmen and the treasures of the city.

Open all year, daily.

YORKSHIRE SCULPTURE PARK
WEST YORKSHIRE.
BRETTON HALL. 1 MILE (1.5KM) FROM JUNCTION 38 M1
TEL: 01924 830302

▶ The sculpture park has pioneered the siting of sculpture in the open air, organising temporary exhibitions of modern and contemporary sculpture by national and international artists in over 100 acres (40ha) of beautiful parkland. There are changing displays by artists including Barbara Hepworth, Bill Tucker, Barry Flanagan, Bill Turnbull and David Nash. In the adjacent 96-acre (39ha) Bretton Country Park, there is a permanent exhibition of bronze sculptures by Henry Moore.

Open all year, daily. Closed 25–26 & 31 Dec.

gazetteer

THE YORKSHIRE DALES NATIONAL PARK

The Yorkshire Dales is a predominantly limestone landscape covering an area of 680 square miles (1,761sq km) that includes much of the Pennines. Scars of exposed white limestone dot the area, especially to the south where the Great Scar Limestone is most common. Here, notably at Ingleborough, the surface limestone which has been cut through by rainwater lies like great jointed pavements across the fells. On the high ground between the wooded, river-worn dales lie bleak gritstone moors of heather. In the higher western and wetter Pennine uplands, peat covers most of the landscape.

Bilsdale, near Hawnby, is a typical dales landscape

gazetteer

THE YORKSHIRE DALES NATIONAL PARK

The Pennine Way runs through the national park from Airton in the south to Tan Hill on the northern boundary. It passes through the village of Malham on to the sweeping amphitheatre of Malham Cove, with the limestone pavement above and the nearby steep-sided Gothic gorge of Gordale Scar. Passing Malham Tarn, one of the park's few lakes, the path winds around the imposing Pen-y-ghent and north through the village of Hawes in Wensleydale, where the area's famous cheese is produced.

East of the Pennine Way, Ingleborough and the park's highest mountain Whernside together with Pen-y-ghent form the Three Peaks. Ingleborough the most famous of the three, rises from Chapel-le-Dale, and has a hillfort-capped summit where the Iron-Age tribe of the Brigantes tried to resist the Roman advance in Britain. On the mountain's southern slopes lies the awesome chasm of Gaping Gill, the biggest pothole in Britain. Here, Fell Beck plunges down Britain's highest unbroken waterfall into a vast underground cavern.

In the north the square towers of Bolton Castle stand overlooking Wensleydale, a wide-bottomed valley replete with waterfalls in this waterfall-covered district. Above the River Ure, the waters of Hardraw Force plummet from an overhanging lip of Yoredale rock past a cliff of sandwiched stone layers into a rock-strewn pool. James Herriot immortalised this area in his books recounting a vet's life in the dales. These prompted the film and the television series, All Creatures Great and Small. There are also numerous waterfalls in the south, particularly near Ingleton, where Kingsdale Beck tumbles downwards over the limestone staircase of Thornton Force.

There are many attractions to the park, both natural and man made. The show caves, Ingleborough Cave and Stump Cross Caverns, are examples of the extensive water-worn caves which stretch out under the dales. Above ground, knots of stone houses form villages all over

THE YORKSHIRE DALES NATIONAL PARK gazetteer

The extensive ruins of Jervaulx Abbey, once a powerful monastic centre

the district, such as Malham, Grassington, Hawes, Sedbergh and Arncliffe in Littondale, where the original *Emmerdale Farm* was filmed. In medieval times the majority of what is now the park was governed by 10 monasteries which, gathering wealth from sheep farming, were able to build the magnificent abbeys which now stand roofless, gutted skeletons of their former glory. The remains of the once magnificent Bolton Priory which date from this period stand on the southern boundary of the park.

Industry has taken its toll upon the park, with its important rock deposits still being extracted by eight active quarries. Squat lime kilns stand on hill-sides adjacent to old workings in the western fells, showing the importance of limestone to the area in the past. Farming has created the characteristic hay meadows of the dales, with walled fields and neat gritstone barns in Swaledale and the upper parts of Ribblesdale. In the west, the Settle to Carlisle Railway cuts through and is carried over the hills and dales of the national park. The 24-arch Ribblehead Viaduct is, in particular, a must for sightseers travelling along the Three Peaks Walk.

LISTINGS

CONTACTS AND ADDRESSES

TOURIST INFORMATION CENTRES

Barnsley* Tel: 01226 206757
Bedale Open: Apr–Oct. Tue only Nov–Mar. Tel: 01677 424604
Beverley* Tel: 01482 867430
Boroughbridge Open: Apr–Oct. Tel: 01423 323373
Bradford* Tel: 01274 753678
Bridlington* Tel: 01262 673474
Danby Open: Apr–Oct. Weekends only Nov–Mar. Tel: 01287 660654
Doncaster* Tel: 01302 734309
Easingwold Open: Jun–Sep. Weekends only Apr, May, Oct. Tel: 01347 821530
Filey Open: May–Oct. Weekends only Nov–Apr. Tel: 01723 512204
Grassington Open: Apr–Oct. Weekends only Nov–Mar. Tel: 01756 752774
Great Ayton Open: Apr–Oct. Tel: 01642 722835
Halifax* Tel: 01422 368725
Harrogate* Tel: 01423 537300
Hawes Open: Apr–Oct. Tel: 01969 667450
Haworth* Tel: 01535 642329
Hebden Bridge* Tel: 01422 843831
Helmsley Open: Apr–Oct. Weekends only Nov–Mar. Tel: 01439 770173
Holmfirth* Tel: 01484 222444
Hornsea Open: Apr–Sep. Tel: 01964 536404
Horton-in-Ribblesdale* Tel: 01729 860333
Huddersfield* Tel: 01484 223200
Hull* Tel: 01482 223559
Humber Bridge* Tel: 01482 640852
Ilkley* Tel: 01943 60231
Ingleton Open: Apr–Sep. Tel: 015242 41049
Knaresborough Open: Apr–Oct. Tel: 01423 866886
Leeds* Tel: 0113 242 5242
Leyburn* Tel: 01969 623069
Malton Open: Mar–Oct. Mon, Wed, Fri, Sat only Nov–Feb. Tel: 01653 600048
Northallerton Open: Apr–Oct. Wed–Sat only Nov–Mar. Tel: 01609 776864

Pateley Bridge Open: Apr–Oct. Tel: 01423 711147
Pickering* Tel: 01751 473791
Reeth Open: Apr–Oct. Weekends Nov–Mar. Tel: 01748 884059
Richmond* Tel: 01748 850252
Ripon Open: Apr–Oct. Tel: 01765 604625
Rotherham* Tel: 01709 823611
Saltaire* Tel: 01274 774993
Scarborough* Tel: 01723 373333
Scotch Corner Open: Apr–Oct. Tel: 01325 377677
Selby* Tel: 01757 703263
Settle* Tel: 01729 825192
Sheffield* Tel: 0114 273 4671/2
Skipton* Tel: 01756 792809
Sutton Bank Open: Apr–Oct. Weekends Nov–Mar. Tel: 01845 597426
Thirsk Open: Apr–Oct. Tel: 01845 522755
Todmorden* Tel: 01706 818181
Wakefield* Tel: 01924 305000/1
Wetherby* Tel: 0113 247 7253
Whitby* Tel: 01947 602674
Withernsea Open: Apr–Sep. Tel: 01964 615683
York* Tel: 01904 620557 and 621756/7

*Centres marked * are open all year.*

NATIONAL PARK AUTHORITIES

North York Moors National Park Authority
Helmsley. Tel: 01439 770657
Yorkshire Dales National Park Authority
Grassington. Tel: 01756 752748

The AA Hotel Booking Service

This new service provided exclusively for AA personal members is a FREE, fast and easy way to find a place to stay for your short break, business trip or holiday. With your membership number to hand, call the AA Hotel Booking Service on 0990 050505.

INDEX

Adborough 6
The ARC, York 84
Armley Mills Industrial Museum, Leeds 42
Askrigg 29
Aysgarth 6
Aysgarth Falls 29
Bankfield Museum, Halifax 23
Bedale 7
Beningbrough Hall 8
Bempton 7
Beverley 8–9
Bishop Wilton 64
Bishops House, Sheffield 74
Bolling Hall, Bradford 13
Bolton Castle 9
Bolton Priory 11
Boroughbridge 12
Boston Spa 12
Bradford 12–14
Bramham Park 14
Bridlington 15
Brodsworth Hall, Doncaster 19
Brontë Parsonage Museum, Haworth 31
Burnby 64
Burton Agnes Hall 15
Burton Constable Hall 16
Byland Abbey, Coxwold 17
Calderdale Industrial Museum, Halifax 24
Cartwright Hall Art Gallery, Bradford 14
Castle Howard 46, 48
Clapham 16
Cleveland Hills 17
Cliffe Castle Museum & Gallery, Keighley 39
Clifford's Tower, York 85
Colour Museum, Bradford 14
Conisbrough Castle 16
Coxwold 17
Craven Museum, Skipton 75
Dales Countryside Museum Centre, Hawes 30
Danby 18
Dewsbury 18
Doncaster 19
Duncombe Park, Helmsley 32
Easby 19
East Riddlesden Hall, Keighley 39
East Witton 19
Eden Camp Modern History Theme Museum, Malton 46
Egton/Egton Bridge 19
Eureka! The Museum for Children, Halifax 24
Fairfax House, York 86
Flamborough 20
Fountains Abbey & Studley Royal, Ripon 68
Friargate Museum, York 86
Georgian Theatre Royal, Richmond 66
Giggleswick 20
Goathland 20
Gomersal 20
Grassington 21

Great Driffield 23
Green Howards Museum, Richmond 66
Guiseley 23
Hackness 23
Halifax 23–4
Hardraw Force 29
Harewood House & Bird Garden 25
Harlow Carr Botanical Gardens, Harrogate 26
Harrogate 26
Hawes 29, 30
Haworth 30–31
Hebden Bridge 32
Helmsley 32–3
Heptonstall 33
Holmfirth 33
Hornsea 34
Huddersfield 34
Hull 35–6
Humber Bridge 36
Hutton-le-Hole 37
Ilkley 37
Ingleton 38
Jorvik Viking Centre, York 86
Keighley 38
Keighley & Worth Valley Railway & Museum, Haworth 31
Kelham Island Industrial Museum, Sheffield 74
Kilburn 39
Kilnsey 39
Kilnwick Percy 64
Kirby Misperton 39
Kirkham Priory 39
Kirkstall Abbey and Abbey House Museum, Leeds 43
Knaresborough 40
Lastingham 40
Leeds 41–4
Leyburn 44
Linton in Craven 45
Litton 45
Londesborough 64
Lotherton Hall 45
Maister House, Hull 36
Malham 45
Malton 46
Manor House Gallery & Musuem, Ilkley 38
Masham 49
Merchant Adventurers' Hall, York 87
Middleham 49
Middlestown National Coal Mining Museum for England 50
Middleton Colliery Railway, Leeds 43
Moors Centre, Danby 18
Morley 50
Mount Grace Priory, Osmotherley 58
Muker 50
Museum of Army Transport, Beverley 9
National Museum of Photography, Film & Television, Bradford 14
National Park Centre, Aysgarth 7

INDEX

National Park Centre, Grassington 22
National Railway Museum, York 87
Newby Hall & Gardens 51
Norman Manor House, Burton Agnes Hall 16
The North York Moors 52–4
North Yorkshire Moors Railway, Pickering 60–1
Norton Conyers 55
Nostell Priory 55
Oakwell Hall 56–7
Osmotherley 58
Otley 58
Parcevall Hall Gardens 58
Pateley Bridge 59
The Pennines 59
Pickering 60
Piece Hall, Halifax 24
Pocklington 63
Pontefract 65
Red House, Gomersal 21
Reed Organ & Harmonium Museum, Saltaire 70
Reeth 65
Richmond 65–6
Rievaulx Abbey 66
Rievaulx Terrace & Temples 67
Ripley 67
Ripon 68
Robin Hood's Bay 69
Roche Abbey 69
Roman Town, Aldborough 6
Rotherham 69
Royal Armouries Museum, Leeds 43
The Royal Pump Room Museum, Harrogate 26
RSPB Nature Reserve, Fairburn 20
RSPB Nature Reserve, Bempton 7
St Williams College, York 88
Saltaire 70
Scarborough 70–1
Selby 72
Semer Water 29
Settle 72
Sewerby Hall & Gardens, Bridlington 15
Sheffield 72–4
Shibden Hall, Halifax 24
Shipley 75
Skipton 75
Staithes 76
Stokesley 76
'Streetlife' – Hull Museum of Transport 36
Sutton Bank 77–8
Sutton Park 76
Temple Newsam House & Park, Leeds 43
Tetley's Brewery Wharf, Leeds 44
Theakston Brewery Visitor Centre, Masham 49
Thirsk 79
Thornton Abbey 79
Thornton Dale 79
Thwaite Mills, Leeds 44
Todmorden 79
Tolson Memorial Museum, Huddersfield 35
Town Docks Museum, Hull 36
Transperience, Bradford 14
Treasurers' House, York 88
Tropical World, Leeds 44
Wakefield 80
West Burton 81
Wetherby 81
Whitby 82
Wilberforce House, Hull 36
York 83–90
Yorkshire Air Museum, York 90
Yorkshire Carriage Museum, Aysgarth 7
The Yorkshire Dales National Park 91–3
Yorkshire Dales National Park Centre, Clapham 16
Yorkshire Dales National Park Centre, Malham 46
Yorkshire Museum & Gardens, York 90
Yorkshire Sculpture Park 90

ACKNOWLEDGEMENTS

The Automobile Association wishes to thank the following photographers and library for their assistance in the preparation of this book.

The photographs are held in the Association's own library (AA PHOTO LIBRARY) and were taken by:
A Baker 21; P Baker 61, 65, 73; J Beasley 26, 61; S L Day 42; R Eames 81; S Gregory 67, 76; A J Hopkins 33; S & O Mathews 6, 20, 28, 50, 77; J Morrison 9, 10, 27, 29, 51, 53, 56, 58, 64, 71, 79, 82, 91; J Mottershaw 31, 38; R Newton 47, 72, 78, 87, 88; V Patel 54; C Rose 57; D Tarn 30, 40, 49, 69, 75, 93; W Voysey 85; L Whitwam 15, 32; P Wilson 13, 18, 22, 35, 37, 55, 59, 80, 83, 89; T Woodcock 17

Cover photographs
INTERNATIONAL PHOTOBANK: front
J A Tims: front – walkers
S & O Mathews: back – top
P Wilson: back – middle
A J Hopkins: back – bottom